SMALL ISLAND BY LITTLE TRAIN

Small Island by
LITTLE TRAIN

A NARROW-GAUGE ADVENTURE

CHRIS ARNOT

To my wife Jackie, whose support has been steadfast as usual.
And in memory of my mother, Mavis Arnot,
who took me on my first train.

For a night and a day they knew their surroundings, and for a night and a day, skirting the edge of the great Indian Desert on a narrow-gauge railway, they remembered how in the days of their apprenticeship they had come by that road from Bombay. Then the languages in which the names of the stations were written changed, and they launched south into a foreign land, where the very smells were new.

– Rudyard Kipling, 'William the Conqueror'

Published by AA Publishing, a trading name of AA Media Limited,
Fanum House, Basing View, Basingstoke, Hampshire, RG21 4EA, UK.

www.theAA.com

Text © Chris Arnot 2017

The right of Chris Arnot to be identified as author of this work has
been asserted by him in accordance with the Copyright, Designs and
Patents Act 1988.

A CIP catalogue record for this book is available
from the British Library.

ISBN: 978-0-7495-7849-7

Editors: Rebecca Needes and Graham Coster
Art Director: James Tims
Designer: Tracey Freestone
Cover Illustrator: Colin Elgie
Map Illustrator: Emma Metcalfe

Typeset in Bembo Regular 12pt

Printed and bound by CPI Group (UK) Ltd, Croydon CR0 4YY

A05471

CONTENTS

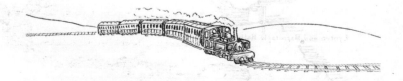

N

0   50   100
MILES

Leadhills and Wanlockhead Railway

South Tynedale Railway

Ravenglass and Eskdale Railway

Welsh Highland Railway

Snowdon Mountain Railway   Ffestiniog Railway

Leek and Manifold Light Railway

Statfold Barn Railway

Talyllyn Railway

Bure Valley Railway

Vale of Rheidol Railway

Southwold Railway

Leighton Buzzard Light Railway

Sittingbourne and Kemsley Light Railway

Lynton and Barnstaple Railway

Romney, Hythe and Dymchurch Railway

PROLOGUE

It was a BBC2 programme called *Full Steam Ahead* that sparked my interest by recreating the journey of a slate train during the 19th century. There was no locomotive involved, however. It didn't even have a driver. There was just a long string of wagons, and a brakeman. The train started up among the mountains of north Wales, and came to a stop 13.5 miles away down at the coast at the bustling harbour of Porthmadog, where that finished slate would be loaded on to boats before sailing off to cover roofs across the world.

And these wagons just rolled downhill the whole way, powered by nothing more than gravity. It wasn't just the men who'd dug out that slate who risked their necks every day. So did those sitting on top of the slate freight, clinging on for grim death. Somehow I doubt those early travellers on that gravity line had much chance to take in the magnificent views on either side. Then again, maybe they just took the scenery for granted.

A few years ago I had visited Blaenau Ffestiniog, at the top of this line, to write about the lost mines that surrounded this little town amidst towering heaps of slate waste. The mountains here were largely man-made. My guide had told me that, unlike the mines, the line that once carried that slate was still open. What's more, you could ride on it, in safety and even comparative comfort. But I had an appointment the following day with a gold miner in a nearby forest, and never had chance to give it a go or even have a look.

A year before that I'd found myself in the very different setting of Hythe, with its narrow high street and imposing promenade overlooking the shingly south coast of Kent. Again I was looking for something lost: a brewery this time – the one that had brewed Mackeson Milk Stout. Yes, Mackeson. They didn't just produce that iron-rich dark-brown ale we all assumed Ena Sharples, Minnie Caldwell and Martha Longhurst were supping in the snug of the Rovers Return. In that Cinque Port on the south coast they produced a wide range of ales, about as far from the setting for *Coronation Street* as it's possible to imagine in this small island.

And in Hythe, apparently, there was another of these odd little railways. Perfectly level, this time, and nothing to do with slate mines, or with British Rail either. It had been set up by a former racing driver with an extremely long name, a hell of a lot of money and a fierce determination to have a railway of his own. Wherever it was, it wasn't immediately evident while I was looking for my lost brewery, and again, I didn't get round to exploring more.

Like most men, I like trains. And, yes, OK, like many men of my generation, I was once a trainspotter. As a boy in the 1950s, I might add. Early sixties at the very latest. Tamworth was the Mecca for many a Midland trainspotter back in my boyhood. We'd become wildly excited when a particularly sleek, named train thundered through. I'm fairly sure I saw *Britannia* at Tamworth and, quite by chance, the *Royal Scot* at either Birmingham New Street or Snow Hill Station while setting out on a rare trip to London with my parents. Somehow it seemed even more exciting than the prospect of lunch at a Lyon's Corner House.

The more adventurous among us would try to 'cab' occasional trains. Climb into the cab of a steam engine, in other words. Not when it was moving, of course, but when it was parked in one of the engine sheds. It was a risky business, involving stealth and a brisk turn of speed in case you were spotted by a member of the railway staff. If caught, you could expect a good telling off at best or the threat of what our parents' generation called 'a thick ear' at worst.

I distinctly remember coming home from a football match at Villa Park in Birmingham at dusk on a Saturday in the days when boys could stand on that imposingly steep Spion Kop known as the Holte End for a shilling (5p). With me were two older lads who bragged that they were going to climb into some sheds near the ground in Aston and then clamber into as many cabs as they cared to. They'd calculated that staff would be thin on the ground at that time on a weekend evening. All the same, I was expected to act as look-out. I was the youngest, after all, and there was to be no arguing. With that, they were off over the fence leaving me out on the pavement for what seemed like an eternity. One minute I'd be glancing this way and that, eyes peeled for approaching police officers; the next I'd be focusing one of those eyes on a hole in the fence, trying to work out where the hell my so-called friends had got to. When, eventually, they jumped back on to the pavement, they were bursting with bragging rights. Never shut up about the engines that they'd 'cabbed' all the way home.

By the time the Golden Age of Steam had finally been shunted into the sidings, though, I was at university, and had long since put behind me memories of standing on platforms with other boys, routinely underlining numbers in a book called a 'ref'.

In due course I became a journalist, and more often than not I would travel to my assignments by train. A series on rugby league towns for the travel editor of the *Guardian*, for example, allowed me to truffle out the distinctive landmarks and institutions that hadn't been flattened by ring roads, housing estates or shopping precincts. Easier in Huddersfield and Halifax than in Salford and Wigan. Yes, there were delays by train, but then there were also traffic jams on the motorways. At least you could work on the train. Mind you, the car was the only option when you had to get to somewhere so remote that Dr Richard Beeching, the physicist who experimented on British Rail, had long ago had the branch line ripped up.

Even the post-Beeching main line had its moments, good as well as bad. Apart from stunning coastal runs from the west coast of Scotland to the southwest of England to the heart of Wales, I'd once spent a joyous evening on the Penistone Line Blues Train from Huddersfield to Sheffield. There was rhythm as well as blues and, on the return journey, couples were jiving in the aisles and the corridors between carriages. A marked contrast, to be sure, from the entire night I once spent aboard an Intercity 125 when it broke down just outside Milton Keynes shortly before the break-up of British Rail. What joy it was to peer out of the window at dawn and spot a concrete cow – or maybe I was dreaming by then. But I certainly wasn't dreaming when another train finally arrived to pick us up and first-class passengers grumpily emerged from keeping warm, like tramps on a park bench, under complimentary copies of the *Telegraph*.

Now, if there's one thing most journalists like, it's eccentricity. The word itself means 'away from the centre', or not the standard way of doing things. It was what had inspired much of my writing for newspapers and, subsequently, the travel and research I'd done for the books I'd written about lost mines, lost breweries and even lost cricket grounds all over Britain. And this BBC2 film of the gravity railway in north Wales had rekindled my memories of that strange little town at the top of the line, surrounded by some of the most stunning countryside in the UK, yet crouched amidst a weird, man-made landscape where sheep grazed on the steep and narrow ledges of spoil tips, grassed over in parts. This was certainly a long way from the centre and the standard in every sense.

But there was something else eccentric about this railway – indeed, the reason why it existed at all. It all had to do with the distance between the rails. At this point, we should get down to brass tacks: gauge the gauge, you might say. All mainline trains, such as the ones that had conveyed me to those rugby league towns and the revellers on the Blues Train, run on tracks that are 1,435 millimetres apart. That's 4ft 8½in in real money. Neither the railway pioneer George Stephenson nor the great engineer Isambard Kingdom Brunel dealt in metric measurements. In fact, Brunel originally settled on a gauge of 7ft 1¼in to give his Great Western Railway more stability.

There are various theories about why Stephenson settled on 4ft 8in. In one on-line debate somebody suggested it is 'the distance between the neck and ankles of a damsel in distress'. I'm more inclined to believe the theory that Stephenson was influenced by the width of the horse-drawn wagons that preceded his invention. He was, after all, a practical engineer, and would have been aware that the tracks in the mud left by wagons and carts throughout our history have mostly been around 4ft 8in.

And that additional half inch? Well, here's one suggestion that seems plausible: 'As locomotives grew larger, and required six wheels, there were problems on curves and it proved easier to push the rails out the extra half inch than to adjust the wheels.' Anyway, it was Stephenson's 4ft 8in, first used on the Stockton and Darlington line and then widened by half an inch on the Liverpool and Manchester Railway, that towards the end of the 19th century became the standard. London Tube trains, the HST, Virgin Pendolinos, the *Flying Scotsman*, the *Brighton Belle*, Eurostar: all run on what is now universally referred to as standard gauge. I'm sure the railway enthusiasts among you will have more detailed knowledge on the subject, but standard gauge is not the subject of this book.

There is, after all, a lot that standard-gauge trains can't do. They can't go up or down steep gradients. They can't cope with sharp bends. That makes a lot of places – indeed, whole landscapes – inaccessible to trains. But if you narrow the gauge…

A narrow gauge made railways more flexible. Building a tunnel is really expensive. Narrow-gauge trains could hug the contours of hilly countryside, get around those hills, and even mountains, without having to go through them. What's more, their lighter weight meant they could make it up steeper gradients than their standard-gauge counterparts, and the track and infrastructure like bridges and viaducts could be built more cheaply. That's why most of them were also

The loop at Agony Point at Tindharia on the Darjeeling Himalayan Railway, 1880s

The Chemin de fer Montreux–Glion–Rochers-de-Naye railway at the small village of Caux, Switzerland in winter, 1908

called a 'light railway'. No wonder they caught the attention of the mine-owners in North Wales.

Narrow-gauge railways came into their own from the 19th century as a way of reaching the places that other railways couldn't reach. When the economic case for the railway was marginal, the narrow-gauge option often made the difference in it getting built at all. They wound up through the Himalayas to transport members of the British Imperial ruling class to remote Indian hill stations in places such as Darjeeling and Shimla to escape the summer heat. They were built up mountains in Switzerland to take tourists to the very summit of the Jungfrau and other lofty destinations, using a remarkable rack-and-pinion system (all cog wheels and teeth) to enable the little locomotive to cling to the track on such a precipitous gradient. During World War I little narrow-gauge lines were built across the last few miles from the main railhead to the frontline, to take many a British 'Tommy' to his death or mutilation in the trenches of northern France. They were even built by Scottish lairds to take their guests from the shooting lodge out onto the grouse moor.

But narrow-gauge railways, you will discover, vary considerably – and not just in their engines, rolling stock, scenery they pass through and reasons for existence. Down at track level, the rails can be anything from 15in apart to twice as wide. Plus a bit more in some cases. There are also various gauges in between 15in and 3ft 6in, and one or two outside that range.

The Padarn Railway in north Wales, which closed in 1961, was 4ft wide, and still regarded as narrow-gauge. Some would put the same label on the Wells and Walsingham Light Railway, although it only has a gauge of 10in. And a quarter. When does a narrow-gauge line become a miniature? Discuss. But not here, if you don't mind.

And that little railway in north Wales, built on a continuous gradient so that its slate wagons could trundle themselves all the way from the mine down to the port, was where it all started. The man who transformed the line, and originated the narrow-gauge railway as we know it, was Charles Easton Spooner, who dominated the Ffestiniog Railway Company from 1856 until 1886. Faced with a growing volume of traffic from the booming slate mines, and the difficulty its first generation of little steam engines were having hauling its increasingly heavy trains up its arduous gradient, Spooner wanted to fend off competition from those seeking alternative routes for the transportation of slate. Eventually he turned to the great Glaswegian railway engineer Robert Francis Fairlie to design a loco capable of pulling greater loads. Such newfangled technology had never been tried on a narrow-gauge line before. Most of the leading designers of the day declared it to be unworkable.

Fairlie and Spooner proved them wrong, albeit only after the line had been re-laid with heavier steel rails. A 'Double Fairlie' – a revolutionary double-ended

A gravity slate train at Dduallt on the Ffestiniog Railway in the days before preservation

Livingston Thompson, *one of the Ffestiniog Railway's patent Double Fairlie locomotives*

locomotive with two fireboxes and two chimneys, effectively two engines joined back-to-back – worked wonders. The first was called *Little Wonder*. In February 1870 railway engineers from around the globe gathered in Porthmadog to see its first trials. Observers from the Denver and Rio Grande Railroad were there. Russians, too. They were there to witness the first most powerful and sophisticated steam engine yet to run on a line just under 2ft wide. It wouldn't be the last. *Little Wonder* and the Double Fairlies were the making of not only the Ffestiniog but narrow-gauge railways everywhere. Over 300 went on to be built, and Charles Spooner became a narrow-gauge evangelist.

Many years later, after World War II, the man who led the way in clearing the long-disused slate line and pioneered its transformation into a magnet for tourists, was one Alan Pegler. I liked the sound of Pegler, a man of ample girth who helped to earn his way out of subsequent bankruptcy by impersonating Henry VIII at the Tower of London no fewer than 700 times. He had lost the family fortune, apparently, by purchasing the *Flying Scotsman* from British Rail and saving it for posterity. Yes, that *Flying Scotsman* – the one rolled out recently after prolonged restoration to draw large crowds to the sides of lines and even larger ones to stations where it has paused to let off steam. Pegler had shipped it to America, only to discover that it was banned as a fire hazard in quite a few states.

Those slate mines up around Blaenau Ffestiniog; that brewery down on the south coast at Hythe; that lovely old cricket ground in the middle of Hastings I'd written about that had disappeared under a hideous shopping precinct: they've all long since gone, along with many another. Mackeson won't be coming back to southern England any more than slate mining will return to North Wales, lead mining to Cumbria or deep-shaft coal mining to anywhere in the UK. For them it's over.

But what was beginning to intrigue me about narrow-gauge railways was that they weren't over. Far from it. They may have had their past in that same very different Britain that relied on mining and heavy industry for its wealth, or in the whims of wealthy racing drivers from a vanished era of glamour and débutantes. And, in some cases, they may have lain dormant for decades as the post-industrial realities set in. They ought to have been as an anachronistic as a crumbling cricket ground up against a shopping precinct. But they were still here. Against the odds, it seemed, they'd even made a comeback.

It was when I discovered that there was even a narrow-gauge railway just an hour's train ride away from where I live that I really got interested. Coventry Station is on the West Coast main line. Ask most of the young people peering into their phones or laptops in the Starbucks on Platform One about the Great Train

Robbery and they would assume it was the price of a ticket on a peak-time Virgin express to London that could have you pulling into Euston in exactly an hour. Coventry is where you go to catch a Pendolino to Glasgow, or, if you have real stamina, a CrossCountry train all the way to Penzance.

But this Sunday morning in that Starbucks, I lugged my 'small Americano' served in the usual brimming mug the size of a small bucket to look at the departures screen for the time of the next London Midland service southbound to the town closest to the spot where the Great Train Robbery of 1963 had actually taken place. The 9.44, that's what I wanted, calling at every station in between: Rugby, Long Buckby, Northampton, Wolverton…

I was going in search of a little line whose track was half the width of the main line and had been laid down using rails salvaged from the Western Front. Now, why would a narrow-gauge railway be needed in an attractive market town in Middle England full of commuters who travel into London every day? Something to do with the quarries and the brickworks, in the days when the town's sand was apparently highly sought-after. That was all I knew.

Soon this modern electric commuter train with its sliding doors and strip lighting was swishing into Milton Keynes Central, two stops before mine. This time around, you'll be glad to hear, we did not break down and have to spend the whole night aboard and wake up to hallucinations of concrete cows. We pulled into my destination bang on time. Leighton Buzzard.

But this was just the beginning of a much longer journey to some of the most distant parts of our shores – a long way from the centre, in every sense. I wanted to find out how many little trains there were around the edges of the United Kingdom and, above all, how and why on earth they were still there – and ride on them. And so began a narrow-gauge adventure around this small island.

1

MADE OUT OF BRICKS

The Leighton Buzzard Railway

The cab that picked me up at Leighton Buzzard station neatly by-passed the town centre, crossed the flower-bedecked bridge over the Grand Union Canal, and dropped me on the outskirts up a driveway on what looked to be just another modern suburban housing estate. Beyond was a narrow path leading to a station very different from those on the main line, with their serve-yourself ticket machines, automatic barriers, electronic timetables and corporate coffee bars.

Platform One was lined with rustic-looking benches and backed by a dazzling array of bluebells and red tulips. Across the narrow tracks, the benches on the opposite platform were dwarfed by horse chestnut trees in full bloom, each five-fingered leaf seemingly drooping under the weight of white candles. Beyond was a public park. All it needed to complete the scene was a cricket match.

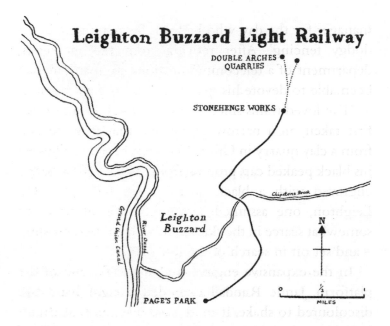

At Page's Park's temporary ticket office the man in front of me had just put in an order for ten adults, nine children... 'Oh, yes, and one senior, please.' The female volunteer had to do rather a lot of prodding of the computer screen before tentatively asking for £136.63, and then remembering that there should be a discount for what might be termed a bulk buy. Then she could take my somewhat more modest order for one return ticket on the 12.20 to Stonehenge Works.

Someone had gone missing. 'She's lost her man,' said Vicki, the booking-office clerk, gesturing towards a somewhat agitated woman. 'Could you go and see if he's in the gents?' she asked Mervyn Leah, the duty manager for the day, who had just been 'fixing a bit of dodgy fencing'. After retiring from the marketing department of a telecommunications company, he had been able to devote his spare time to his great passion:

'I've loved trains since I was a small child, and I was first taken on a narrow-gauge line that went to and from a clay quarry in Ufton, Warwickshire.' He adjusted his black peaked cap, proudly fronted by a yellow badge engraved with a black buzzard – a buzzard called Leighton, one assumed, although birds of prey are somewhat scarce in the skies in this part of Bedfordshire – and set off in search of the lost man.

In the expansive engine shed at the far end of the platform, Jamie Randall extended a right hand too discoloured to shake. It must have been all that Brasso he'd been applying to the gleaming interior parts of ancient steam trains. 'This one's 137 years old,' he proclaimed.

'Almost as old as Duncan,' chimed in his mate Liam, with a cheeky glance in the direction of another volunteer wearing blue overalls and sporting a white beard. Facial hair of various shades of grey, or out-and-out white, seemed to be *de rigeur* for volunteers of a certain age. As for Liam and Jamie, they hardly looked old enough to grow beards of any colour. 'I'm nearly 15,' said Liam, who was sporting a so-far unsullied white shirt under his overalls.

'And I was 15 last week,' said Jamie. 'I just drifted along here when I was eight.' It was, by all accounts, a big moment in his life when he became strong enough to shift a points lever unaided.

Jamie and Liam were perhaps the most polite, friendly and obliging teenagers I've ever met as they showed me the shed harbouring some of the railway's rolling stock. Here was *Chaloner*, built in Caernarfon in the late 1870s and used to transport slate from the quarries of North Wales. And here was *Shishta*, built in Burton-on-Trent in 1921 and discovered in India by an ICI executive in 1963 – buried in the undergrowth, apparently, with a washing line attached to its impressive funnel. All brass and copper fittings had to be replaced. A similarly neglected engine from a sugar plantation in South Africa was being lovingly restored and painted by one of several former engineers who have joined the volunteers here since retirement.

'Would you like to drive a steam train?' I asked the teenagers.

'Yes,' said Liam, unhesitatingly.

'I'm more of a diesel person,' Jamie assured me.

The very idea of a tilting Virgin Pendolino that could travel at over 120mph would have been cast in the realms of science fiction when the Leighton Buzzard Light Railway was first laid down. Nearly 100 years ago it was one of the narrow-gauge lines threaded through this island to transport raw materials, in the days when the birthplace of the Industrial Revolution was still coated with the smoke and dust of factories, mills and mines. Quarries, too, in the case of Leighton Buzzard. The town's sand was once so highly regarded that it was used in the construction of the Crystal Palace, and the line was created specifically to transport sand from the many quarries hereabouts to the Stonehenge Brickworks, so named because its products were expected to last for an extremely long time.

On this Sunday in early summer the Leighton Buzzard Railway was running as usual. Not for the transportation of sand, but for the conveyance of those who wanted to travel back in time to the days when trains trundled rather than sped.

The two rival companies that co-operated to have this line laid out in 1919 soon worked out that sand and steam trains didn't mix. Those fine grains tended to get into 'the works', and smoke from the funnel contaminated the sand. So they moved over to diesels made up the road in Bedford. The preserved railway still had two of them, one of which dated back to 1922.

Although it looked to be of similar vintage, the Beaudesert diesel pulling us out of Page's Park any time now had been made by Alan Keef of Ross-on-Wye not much more than 20 years ago. The driver, John Hopper, drove mainline trains for London Midland all week and narrow-gauge engines on Sundays and Bank Holidays. 'All of our holidays and day trips as a family were by train,' he recollected. 'We didn't have a car. So I got into rail travel from a very young age.' At the age of 10, and evidently showing symptoms of summer-holiday boredom, he was told by his mother to 'sod off and do something more interesting than sitting around the house', as she pointed up the road to Page's Park and gave him enough money for four rides, associate membership and a sausage roll from the cafe. He was hooked.

But surely there was a difference between driving here on a 2ft-wide track and on a mainline track that was 4ft 8in? And a half?

'They're a world away,' he confirmed – not least because the Beaudesert could do about 10mph flat out, while a London–Midland train is capable of 110. If, that is, it didn't have to keep stopping at the many stations between London Euston and Birmingham New Street. 'Far more money has been invested in the big trains, so it's a more automated process. They have gated level crossings. Here we have to cross open roads and expect the cars to give way.' It was nearly 12.20pm, and John had to clamber into his cab.

In a somewhat crowded front carriage the majority of the nine children for whom tickets were being bought when I arrived were already sucking the last drops of some sugary drink through straws in transparent plastic containers. A toddler was trying to swig water from a bottle almost as big as himself. A teenage girl in startling silvery slip-ons opposite me was taking selfies. Well, the view out of the window was a classic slice of England in mid-May. No cricket match, admittedly, but there was a croquet club next door to the park. As John set us in motion with a toot of the horn that seemed likely to send a tremor through the bird life of Leighton Buzzard, the white-clad players raised their mallets in unison.

We were off.

That horn would sound many a time on the journey we had just embarked on. Sometimes it was to warn drivers on the C-class roads to give way. At others it was to forewarn those on busier byways that guards would soon be leaping from the train to bar their way. Each time, the eyes and mouth of three-year-old James White seemed to open even wider. Sitting in the front seat, he had been entranced since we set forth, much to the pleasure of his grandparents. 'He's loved narrow-gauge trains ever since we took him on the Lynton and Barnstaple,' said Grandad. 'I have a model train at home that runs around the garden,' he confided. He also sported a white beard.

James's face widened to incredulity as he pointed upwards and proclaimed: 'The trees are coming over us!' Although we were still very much in the realms of suburbia, this was the most verdant time of year and the trees lining the route did appear to be linking leaves overhead. John the driver was slowing down at times to snap off twigs that were intruding into his cab. 'He needs a helping hand,' suggested James.

'I think he could do with some secateurs,' said Grandad. As the foliage began to thin out, he beamed at his grandson and hissed, 'Now we're picking up steam.' Well, diesel power, anyway.

Considering the origins of the line, it seemed ironic that the modern housing estates we were passing through had not been built with bricks made from Leighton Buzzard sand. There were still a couple of sand companies locally, and, indeed, a roofing tile factory, but since the demise of Stonehenge, no brickworks.

Needless to say, the surrounding landscape would have looked very different back in 1919 when the line was somewhat hurriedly laid down to offset an alarming rise in costs at the end of World War I. Before it, most British sand had been imported from what the propagandists called 'poor little Belgium' once it was occupied by German troops. When supplies were cut off, the British government turned from Belgium to Bedfordshire, and Leighton Buzzard in particular. As the Leighton Buzzard Light Railway chairman Terry Bendall had told me a few days earlier, 'Ministers said to the sand companies: "You get the sand to the [main line] railway anyway you like – by horse and cart, steam, lorries or whatever. We'll pick up the road repair bill."'

Which was?

'A thousand pounds a month.'

That was a hell of a lot of money in those days. But then the roads were hardly in good nick to start with, and the sheer weight of sand piled on to tyre-less wheels took a terrible toll.

'As soon as the war was over,' Terry went on, 'the sand companies were told that they had to pay for road maintenance.'

Out of the question at those prices, I should have thought.

'It was. So they went across to the Western Front and took some narrow-gauge track.'

Light railways made an important contribution to the war effort, and were used for the supply of ammunition and stores to the trenches, the transport of troops and the evacuation of the wounded. Hundreds of narrow-gauge locomotives were built by companies such as Hunslet, Kerr, Stuart, Davenport, Motor Rail and Baldwin. So presumably the Leighton Buzzard sand companies managed to get their hands on one or two spare engines as well as the track?

'Oh, yes. They had armour-plated ones on this line. One of them wasn't scrapped until 1959.'

By that time the railway was reaching the end of the line, so to speak. The shift from rail to road transport was underway in all sections of industry, and sand was no exception. Road surfaces were considerably more resilient, and the lorries that travelled over them took less of a toll than their predecessors from 40 years previously.

And so it came to pass that, by the mid-1960s, the Leighton Buzzard narrow-gauge railway had run its course as a means of transporting sand. But there was no shortage of enthusiastic volunteers prepared to

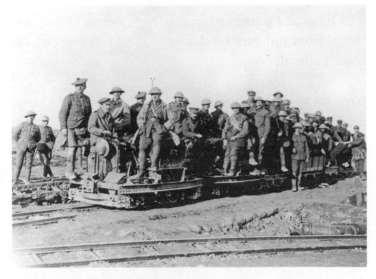

WWI British soldiers on a light railway at the Western Front

A Leighton Buzzard Railway loco loaded with sand from Churchways Quarry passes over the level crossing at Eastern Way in 1977

take it on as a preserved line. Which meant that it was passed from industrial to leisure usage without a break. Most unusual.

Back on the 12.20, we had just passed the site of what used to be Marley's Tile Works and were fast approaching Marley's Bank, where we were going to head downhill fast. Faster than usual, anyway. The gradient was 1 in 25.

Like so many narrow-gauge railways, the line was laid on the cheap. The sand companies couldn't call upon navvies to blast holes and dig tunnels. They had to go with the flow of the landscape around the outskirts of the town, and it goes without saying that there were far fewer vehicles on the roads in those days. Nearly a century later stopping the traffic at fairly regular intervals is something of an occupational, or rather recreational, hazard for those who volunteer for guard duty. We'd already passed the Stanbridge Road gateless level crossing; now we were approaching another one at the somewhat busier Hockliffe Road. A prolonged blast on the horn heralded the descent from either end of the train of two guards wearing yellow jackets and waving red flags. True to form, one looked to be a teenager, and the other had a beard best described as a whiter shade of grey.

Trains had the right of way here, and the vast majority of motorists had been prepared to pull up and wait. Some even waved. There had been exceptions in the past, however – notably a BMW driver who ploughed into a steam train fast enough to push it off the line, and claimed later he didn't see the flag. Luckily, there were no injuries.

After two more crossings, the train veered sharply to the right through an angle of about 90 degrees. From the rear carriage you could have easily taken a photograph of the engine.

Now we were out into open countryside, cow parsley frothing by the side of the line as we whooshed past. To the right was a colourful wildflower meadow; to the left a flock of sheep harbouring what seemed a disproportionate number of black lambs fled to the far end of the field, much to the joy of young James. Suddenly, at somewhere called Heath and Reach, an enormous wind turbine loomed into view. 'That's the biggest in Britain,' said Grandad. Twice the height of All Saints' Church spire in Leighton Buzzard, apparently. No sooner had we pulled into the station of the old Stonehenge Works than the kids disappeared into the cafe to purchase refills.

I found myself standing beside a huge pile of coal that looked as though it had waited a while for a steam train to turn up. Next to it was the railway's archivist, William Shelford, pointing out for me where the brickworks' chimney used to be before it was demolished in 1985 – by Fred Dibnah, no less, the celebrity steeplejack who made regular appearances on the telly. Still standing, however, was a rather attractive stable block built in 1918 by prisoners-of-war and used to house the horses once kept for work in the quarries. It was now home to another substantial railway workshop.

John had turned around our engine and offered me the chance to ride in the cab with him and one of the guards. Once again, he gave that hooter some toot. No, he didn't have to press a brass dial or pull a copper chain. He simply yanked on what looked rather like a length of sawn-off washing line.

On the return journey I found myself spending more time looking at levers and dials than I did gazing towards the Chilterns and trying to pick out the chalk engraving of the White Lion of Whipsnade. Most passers-by waved to us. The exceptions were a jogger who looked so exhausted he was almost bent double, and a group of youths who obviously thought themselves too cool to wave at trains. 'It's good when kids are waving at you because you know their hands are empty,' said John, recalling the days when a council estate alongside the line tended to be the source of occasional missiles hurled in his direction. 'There was one particularly nasty occasion when they seemed to have discovered a lot of dog poo.' That lunchtime, as we chugged and tooted past the estate, one little boy was running along waving and grinning.

Having crested the summit of Marley's Bank at full throttle, we were soon getting a glimpse once more into the back gardens of sedate suburbia. Lines of washing were hanging limp on a breeze-free day.

Children, some in crash helmets, were bouncing high on enormous trampolines. A few conservatories were a-glint in the sun of early afternoon. Those sheds, though, looked a bit on the dinky side – too small to harbour much more than a lawn mower and some garden tools.

I suspected the men of the Leighton Buzzard Light Railway would have more substantial sheds than these and, when they weren't at the railway, they'd be doing what Englishmen have always done in those oily lairs with spanner-strewn benches and shelves lined with jam jars full of nails, nuts and bolts. They'd be repairing and building and sometimes inventing. Chairman Terry, a former woodwork and metalwork teacher, had already told me he shared a shed with his son for some scale modelling.

Around 120 of the Railway's 400 or so members were involved week-in, week-out, and the previous year they had put in around 25,000 hours of volunteer time. Some of them had also had to dig deep into their pockets to raise the nigh-on £400,000 required for professional builders rather than volunteers to erect the new Museum Gateway station at Page's Park. (It helped that one member is a retired banker and felt able to chip in 130 grand.) By the time you read this, Museum Gateway will be up and running and, as the name suggests, will incorporate a museum as well as a ticket office.

And every Tuesday, come rain, hail or shine, volunteers gathered at the Big Shed at the end of Page's

Rishra at Leedon, waiting to return to Page's Park, 1974

Park's platform to focus their skills or their muscle on carriages and engines built a hell of a long time ago. 'Believe me, it can be damn cold in that shed in the middle of February,' said Terry. 'I remember someone shouting out one particularly freezing Tuesday morning, "Are we having fun yet, chaps?"'

It was quite a warm, early-summer afternoon and there was time for a browse around the town before heading back to the mainline station. There were plenty of handsome 18th- and 19th-century buildings including Leighton Middle School, where, I discovered, Mary Norton, the creator of *The Borrowers*, had once lived. All was quiet this Sunday afternoon. In the Black Lion, which turned out to be CAMRA's Bedfordshire Pub of the Year, with no fewer than eight cask-conditioned beers gushing forth from hand pumps, food was restricted to samosas, pasties and pork pies.

A formidable pie of ample circumference was duly delivered, with a knife protruding from its centre like Excalibur from the stone. A local folk band launched into an impromptu gig, making me want to stay even longer in this haven off the High Street. Alas, I was still only half way through my pie when already the 3.15 back to Coventry was beckoning. The landlady kindly wrapped up the remains in greaseproof paper and I reluctantly set forth for the station, feeling rather like a kid leaving a birthday party with a slice of cake in a napkin. All I needed was a balloon.

On the way home, between surreptitious nibbles of pork pie, I reflected that my narrow-gauge journey would now be taking me to parts of this small island not nearly so easily accessible as Leighton Buzzard, but getting to them and riding on more quirky, even rather magical little lines like this one would be a lot more fun than working in an engine shed in mid-winter.

2

PAPERING OVER
THE CRACKS

The Sittingbourne and
Kemsley Light Railway

We shall never know what Sir John Betjeman would have made of smartphones. The former poet laureate died in 1984 when 'mobiles' were the size of house-bricks and strictly for verbal communication. Still, I suspect that he would be tickled pink to know that so many of those born long after his death routinely pull out their phones to take pictures of his statue as it peers upwards at the magnificent vaulted roof at St Pancras Station. A group of Chinese students were getting him into focus as I rushed off to catch the 12.27 – not to Paris, alas, but to Sittingbourne in Kent.

St Pancras is the most stunning station in London. Along with its adjoining hotel, it seems to rise majestically above the humdrum clamour and congestion of the Euston Road like a fairytale palace

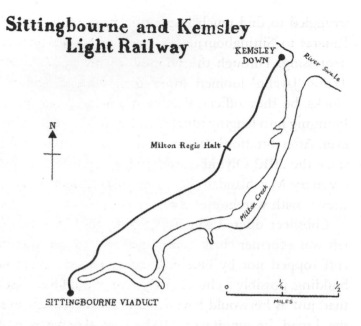

offering passage to magic lands. To be credited with saving it from demolition is the sort of tribute most poets could only dream of. (Edward Thomas may have immortalised Adlestrop as a byword for an English rural idyll, but it was one of many rural stations closed on the orders of British Rail technocrat Dr Richard Beeching in the 1966, nearly 50 years after Thomas's death at the Battle of Arras.)

One of many things we *do* know about Betjeman is that he loved railways. He even turned the line from Baker Street through the suburbs of northwest London into poetry in *Metroland*, his 1973 programme for the BBC. Over 40 years on, I suspect, he would have struggled to find much inspiration in the line from St Pancras to Sittingbourne. The first part is particularly depressing. Through the window of my Southeastern Trains 'Javelin' loomed more than enough concrete blocks, be they offices, flats or multi-storey car parks. Plunging into lengthy tunnels was almost a relief for the eyes. After Stratford 'International', as we must call it since the 2012 Olympics, something unusual appeared: greenery. Marshland, to be more precise, albeit marshes strewn with warehouses, flyovers and pylons.

Ebbsfleet offered something different. Over to the left was a former chalk quarry that looked like a white cliff topped not by bluebirds but a rather handsome building, possibly a church. Betjeman would have liked that, just as he would have revelled in the bridge over the broad, brown River Medway at Rochester and, perhaps, the converted oast house overlooking the station at Rainham. If that seemed like an indication that the hoppy land of rural Kent beckoned, it was an illusion shattered when the Javelin, having hurtled here from St Pancras, glided into Sittingbourne bang on time at 13.21.

Waiting to meet me was Paul Best, who had grown up here but had no illusions about this part of his former home town – or indeed about the narrow-gauge railway that it harboured.

'I can't pretend that it's the most scenic line,' he cautioned. 'But it has the real feel of an industrial railway.' As a trustee and one of between 60 and 80 active volunteers, Paul was sporting a peaked cap fronted by the initials SKLR (Sittingbourne and Kemsley Light Railway). He was also lugging a bulging *Star Wars* carrier bag in his right hand. Like me, he had just come down from London. From Victoria rather than St Pancras, mind you, because that was where he worked. Now 43 and a railway man to his bones, he had graduated from the signal box at Sittingbourne main line to the much busier terminal just north of the river, before becoming a strategic planner on the main line. He lived in Hampshire but travelled back to his old home town at regular intervals to do a stint as guard or station master on the SKLR. An affable character, he had a good sense of humour and none of the earnestness that some sneerers associate with railway 'enthusiasts'.

You would need some enthusiasm, or at least commitment, to stick with the Sittingbourne and Kemsley over the past 20 years or so. It has had more than its fair share of problems, as we shall see. You would also need some commitment to *find* the station if you didn't have someone like Paul alongside you. We passed by substantial outposts of McDonald's, KFC, Homebase and many another of the usual suspects – sorry, household names – before coming across something less corporate at the far end of a sizeable retail park.

A row of substantial slabs was covered by an extensive and colourful mural of the railway that was awaiting us at the top of a steep, grassy embankment. Up some recently installed and glossily painted steps we climbed before arriving at what you might, if you were being ironic, call the Sittingbourne Viaduct 'terminal'. St Pancras suddenly seemed a very, very long way away. Here was little more than a platform, and a corrugated iron shed – a replacement for the original ticket office, which had been burnt down.

Here was an all-too-evident contrast: on one side, the hard work and dedication of the volunteers – opticians, surveyors, postmen and mainline railway workers among them; on the other, the moronic negativity of the vandals who have plagued this line. There used to be another station, or 'halt', between here and Kemsley. It was called Milton Regis, and there it wasn't just the buildings that were burnt down; the platform was smashed to pieces. 'Who would do that?' I found myself musing out loud.

'Someone with a lot of time and patience,' said Paul before adding drily: 'And a crowbar.'

Milton Regis was once threaded by streets of terraced housing. Now it housed a branch of Asda. 'Before the halt was closed down, you could get off there, pick up some shopping and catch the next train back,' Paul recalled. Now there was no stop between Sittingbourne and Kemsley Down. But then it was not much more than two miles away.

At one time the line would have carried on another three miles to Ridham Docks beyond. The tracks were originally laid down on the orders of 19th-century newspaper publisher Edward Lloyd, to link the paper mills of Sittingbourne and Kemsley with the means of waterborne transport to London. Originally a horse-drawn tramway, the line was converted to a railway by his third son Frank in the early 20th century. One of the SKLR's claims to fame is that it still has the original engines running on part of the original line with the original rolling stock. Its survival as a piece of narrow-gauge heritage can be traced back to Bowaters, who took over the mills from the Lloyd family in 1936 and handed over the track to the Locomotive Club of Great Britain in 1969 when the line could no longer be justified economically.

One of those venerable chuffers, *Melior*, a beautifully restored vision in green, red, black and highly polished brass, was puffing towards us now. Some of the children enjoying the early stages of the school holiday were wildly excited. A lady with a large yellow flower protruding from her bodice was not. 'We're from Stoke-on-Trent and we've been to a wedding,' said Liz Lees, whose husband Ian, a former electrician in the Merchant Navy, was taking photographs of *Melior* with an impressive-looking camera. 'He's a "buff",' Liz sighed. 'We've been to all the Welsh narrow-gauge lines and God knows how many others. Mind you, we do go to Ibiza now and again. There are no railways there,' she added dreamily.

'Surely,' I suggested, 'you must have some admiration for these beautiful engines and the effort that goes into keeping them going?'

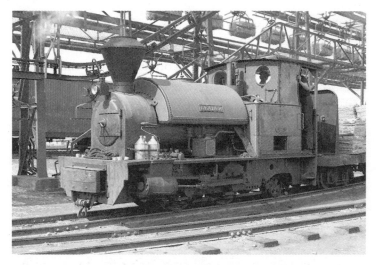

Leader *at Bowaters United Kingdom Pulp & Paper Mills Ltd, Sittingbourne, 1957*

Melior *and* Premier *outside the shed at Bowaters United Kingdom Pulp & Paper Mills Ltd, Sittingbourne, 1969*

'Well, yes, I like them and I even take pictures of them occasionally. Then I forget all about them. But Ian never does. He's building his own small-scale railway at home, and we have a library of railway boots.'

'Did you say books?'

'No, boots. The sort of boots that railway workers wore. They're all over the house – even in the bathroom.'

By now it was time to climb aboard the 14.00 to Kemsley Down. The carriage was of similar vintage to the engine, but its name, *Tom Noakes*, was bestowed far more recently. 'Tom was one of the carriage and wagon engineers here who also worked in the ticket office,' Paul explained. 'Sadly, he died on the job, as it were. He collapsed in the ticket office on the first day after we reopened in 2010.'

Closure had come two years previously, after production had ceased at Sittingbourne Mill and the new Finnish owners, M-real, tried to sell the land. They eventually backed off in the face of a lengthy campaign involving Swale Borough Council and Lord Faulkner, chairman of the Railway Heritage Committee.

This was the second time that the line had endured a prolonged closure. The first had been back in the 1990s, when there was perceived to be a weakness in one of no fewer than 118 spans in the lengthy viaduct over which we were now passing. That problem took two years to sort out. Below the viaduct were the yards of steel fabricators, concrete pipe manufacturers and other industrial companies. The pipes alongside us, once lined with asbestos, used to carry high-pressure steam to the paper works.

Not the prettiest of views, then, as Paul had already conceded. But the children waving out of the window were still excited. Not least a little girl called Alice, whose grandmother proudly proclaimed: 'She told me yesterday that she wanted to be a train driver.'

No longer, it seems, is this an ambition confined to the male of the species. Before we'd set off, I'd managed to catch a quick chat with the train's fire 'man', one Jacqueline Shanks. Despite coming from right-on Bright-on, which has more than its fair share of *Guardian* readers, she preferred to be called a fireman than a firewoman or a fireperson. And she'd no more like to be referred to as a 'fire' than the SKLR's chairman, Liz Fuller, would want to be called a 'chair'. Who said narrow-gauge railways are just 'toys for boys'?

Liz was a senior lecturer at the University of Greenwich, and Jacqueline a freelance surveyor with flexible working hours that allowed her to indulge her passion for railways. 'I've always been interested in steam,' she had told me between shovelling coal and assiduously checking gauges. 'I remember pleading with my parents for my first train set when I was five years old. Funnily enough, my brother wasn't interested in trains.'

Back in the *Tom Noakes* carriage, the view was beginning to improve. We had finally reached the end of the viaduct, past the former gasworks, pipe-works and sewage works. Open country beckoned. Marshland again, but unsullied by warehouses, flyovers and pylons. Yes, it was flat, but that's part of the allure of this comparatively small but infinitely varied island – the great contrasts that it offers in scenery between, say, the steep green hills of Wales and the wide open flatlands of east and southeastern England. You just knew that this marshland was harbouring all kinds of wildlife. 'I've seen a couple of herons this year,' Paul confided as we glanced to the left where the marshes were freshwater. To the right the gulls were swooping and soaring over saltwater marshes.

As Kemsley Down drew nearer, 'England's biggest paper mill' (now owned by D S Smith) hove into view across the reed beds. The journey had taken just 15 minutes. Still, the fare was only seven quid for adults, a fiver for concessions and £3 for children.

Rather than catch the 14.35 back, we stayed to wander around. Time well spent, as it turned out. Kemsley Down was very much the hub of the railway, where the engine shed was located. Not to mention the shop, a small museum and a cafe. We sat outside with cups of tea while the kids made the most of the toy cars, motorbikes and space-hoppers provided, and a large, puce-faced woman, who had seen off most of the contents of a picnic basket before and during the journey, was topping up with a biscuit or three washed down by a Fruit Shoot.

Kemsley Down was growing on me. It had something of the wildness of the marshes, tempered by small pockets of cultivation. The most obvious example of the latter was the delightful little garden, tucked away at the rear of the site and in full summer bloom at the end of July. 'Here we have the insect hotel,' grinned Paul, pointing to a carefully constructed pile of bricks and dry logs with holes drilled into them. 'Over in that far corner is the stag beetle house. I've seen the size of them and, as far as I'm concerned, I hope they stay over there.'

Time to beetle a retreat, perhaps. Enough of this nature study; it was time to get down to business and visit the engine shed. Immediately we stepped over the threshold, the nostrils were assailed by the reassuring aroma of oil. Here we found *Leader* and *Premier*, two of the most venerable locomotives of all, dating back to the opening of the railway line in 1905. One was predominantly green, the other predominantly red. But both had shiny black funnels and frontages as well and, it almost goes without saying, gleaming brass fittings. Both had taken 20 years or more to restore to their full glory but – here's the rub, as they say when reaching for the metal polish – steam engines running on lines like this had to be stripped down every 10 years when their 'boiler ticket' ran out. (A boiler ticket was the official certificate that confirmed that these huge pressurised water boilers, in which the water heated by the burning of coal in the firebox produced the steam to drive the engine's pistons, were safe to operate.)

'*Premier's* boiler is at the North Norfolk Railway being re-tubed,' said Paul. The tubes carried the hot gases from the firebox through the boiler to heat the water.

And *Leader*?

'Should be at work again next week,' he assured me. 'Mind you, its boiler ticket runs out in two years' time.'

Nearby *Alpha* wasn't going to be running any time soon. Hadn't seen a day in service since 1969, apparently. 'We keep her for the parts,' Paul explained. 'Mind you, some of our younger members have now started to do some work on it.'

On the rails just beyond the rear end of the shed was *Unique*. As the name suggests, this engine was a one-off – a standard-gauge loco on narrow-gauge wheels. 'A real monster of a machine, this one,' my guide beamed approvingly. 'Being a paper mill, they didn't want too many sparks flying about. This was one that you could plug in and charge up with enough steam to keep it running for eight hours. Eventually it would run out of puff and you'd have to plug it in again. It's a really impressive engine but, unfortunately, it's been left out in the open for too long.' That explained why there was now a brambly sort of vegetation twirling around the funnel like a garland for past services.

Before catching the return train back to Sittingbourne, I took the opportunity to climb into the cab of *Melior* for a quick chat with its driver, Martin Staniforth, while Jacqueline was returning from the cafe with two mugs of tea. So hot was it here at the sharp end that I might have been more inclined to slurp something chilled. Martin shrugged when I mentioned the heat. 'I was a fireman for four years while training as a driver. I was 17 when I first became involved with this railway, and I'm 49 now. And when I'm not here, I'm repairing diesel carriages. But I'm paid to do that. It's my job,' he said before adding, apropos of nothing: 'I bought a steamroller once.'

'What did your other half say about parking that on the drive?'

'I was nearly married once but it didn't quite work out.'

Steam trains and steamrollers? Well, there was an obvious connection. Boys and toys indeed!

Back in the merciful cool of platform level, I spotted Ian Lees, husband of the long-suffering Liz, taking a brief break from photographing engines. He assured me that he had given up trainspotting at 14 – in the form of taking numbers, anyway. He had, of course, travelled on a fair number of narrow-gauge lines in more recent years, including many more scenic ones than the Sittingbourne and Kemsley. 'But I like this one because it's different. It's industrial and has kept its heritage. Railways are not meant to be pretty; they're meant to work.'

I thought about that as the Javelin hurtled back towards St Pancras, arriving on time again. Shortly before pulling into London's most stunning station, I spotted something I hadn't seen on the way out – a canal basin that looked more appealing than it might have done because it was surrounded by so much urban sprawl. Which made me think again about our best loved poet laureate of the 20th century. The Betjeman statue was still surrounded by phone-focussing students (Japanese this time) as I strolled past on the way to the Betjeman Bar. After paying for a pint with the sort of money that would have bought a leather-bound copy of his collected works in the year of his death, I raised a silent toast. Not to Sir John, who has more than his fair share of admirers, but to those who had kept the Sittingbourne and Kemsley on the rails against the odds.

3

THE 11.15 TO THE
END OF THE WORLD

THE ROMNEY, HYTHE AND
DYMCHURCH LIGHT RAILWAY

Like many a young boy, Jack Howey wanted to be a train driver when he grew up. In other respects, however, 'Jack' had little in common with most other boys. His real name was John Edwards (with an 's') Presgrave Howey, and he had been to Eton. As *The Times* rather euphemistically put it in his obituary in 1963, his parents 'discouraged' him from starting his working life as an apprentice in a loco shed. Instead he felt obliged to join the army. As a Captain during World War I he transferred to the Royal Flying Corps, was shot down behind enemy lines and, after two years in a prisoner-of-war camp, was invalided home via Switzerland.

After the war he became a racing driver, as did his would-be partner in buying or laying down a narrow-gauge line. Count Louis Zborowski not only loved fast cars but, like Howey, he also had an interest in how things worked – railway engines as well as internal combustion engines. Indeed, he built his own railway at his home in Higham Park, Kent. It helped that he had become the fourth richest under-21-year-old in the world in 1911 when his American mother died and bequeathed him £11 million in cash plus seven acres of Manhattan, including several blocks on Fifth Avenue. Agreeing to donate the rolling stock and infrastructure to Howey's proposed project must have seemed like small change.

Zborowski had become intrigued by 15-inch railways, first developed by Sir Arthur Heywood in Derbyshire and now being designed by another celebrated engineer, Henry Greenly, for the model train specialists Bassett-Lowke, and it was at Bassett-Lowke's shop in Holborn that Zborowski ordered two 15in engines. According to J B Snell's book on the Romney, Hythe and Dymchurch line, *One Man's Railway*, the Count was accompanied by the Grand Duke Dmitri Pavlovitch, joint assassin of Rasputin and one of the few Romanovs to escape execution by the Bolsheviks after the Russian Revolution.

A few years later, in 1924, Zborowski's part in Howey's plans came to an abrupt end. He was killed in an accident at the Monza Grand Prix. (Forty years later, incidentally, Ian Fleming took a break from writing James Bond books and penned a children's

Captain Howey and Henry Greenly (who designed the whole railway from locomotives to stations, bridges and coaches) surveying the site of New Romney Station in 1926

SMALL ISLAND BY LITTLE TRAIN

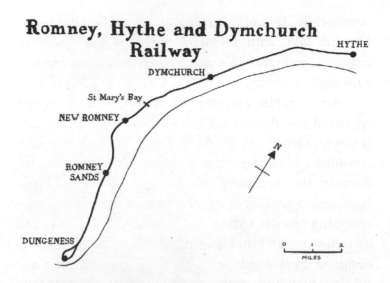

Romney, Hythe and Dymchurch Railway

story called *Chitty Chitty Bang Bang*, based on one of Zborowski's cars. As a youngster, Fleming had watched him race at Brooklands; later he visited Higham Park. Four years after the book's publication, *Chitty Chitty Bang Bang* became a rather successful film, starring Dick Van Dyke.)

Howey was evidently determined to follow his dream, despite the loss of the Count's backing. He even made an unsuccessful bid for the Ravenglass and Eskdale Railway at the other end of England.

It was Henry Greenly who eventually drew his attention to a site much closer to home. He saw the potential for a 15in-gauge line, initially from New Romney to Hythe. The racing driver breezed over to take a look one day in September 1925, and needed no convincing. It had everything: sea views, Romney Marshes and, with Dymchurch and other places in between, enough locals and holidaymakers to provide passengers a-plenty.

After a public enquiry, the Minister of Transport approved the Romney, Hythe and Dymchurch Light Railway Order on 26 May 1926. Work must have continued at some pace under Greenly's management, because the inaugural train from Hythe to New Romney, a distance of just over eight miles, was chugging forth within 14 months. Like all the locomotives, and indeed the carriages, *Hercules* was designed by Greenly at a third of the size of your average mainline steam engine and is described as 'Mountain Class'. As for Dungeness, to which the R, H and D was extended in 1928, it was a place I had always wanted to visit.

So here I was, at the furthest edge of Kent from Sittingbourne: the south coast as opposed to the north. I was staying with a friend in Hastings whose son had played on its evocative and historic cricket ground, now buried under a bog-standard shopping precinct. Hythe, which I'd last visited in search of the remains of the old Mackeson brewery, was a winding, 27-mile drive and, alas, there was no time to revisit that attractive Cinque Port on this sunny Saturday in early September. The gateway to the Romney, Hythe and Dymchurch Railway appeared suddenly on a sharp bend on the edge of town.

ROMNEY, HYTHE & DYMCHURCH R^{LY}
TIME TABLE, from JULY 17th, until further notice.

(timetable with Week-Days and Sundays columns for stations: New Romney, Romney Warren Halt, Holiday Camp, Dymchurch, Burmarsh Road, Botolphs Bridge, Prince of Wales, Hythe)

* Stops to pick up or set down on notice being given at a previous Station.   † Will stop to pick up or set down on request (when completed.)
Conveyances meet all Trains at Hythe for Sandling Junction, Southern Railway, and pick up passengers there for Hythe.
R. H. & D., New Romney Station is directly opposite Southern Railway Station.   Above Time Table is subject to alterations which will be posted at all Stations.
A. These trains will not come into operation until the Ministry of Transport Lighting Regulations have been completed.

ROMNEY, HYTHE & DYMCHURCH RAILWAY CO.,
B. D. BELLAMY, General Manager.

A 1927 timetable and a vintage train ticket

It was the last day of the high season on which the full summer timetable would be available, and the place was buzzing. At least there was a table free in the cafe for a quick coffee with the railway's general manager, Danny Martin. As I was beginning to sense with narrow-gauge railways, there was a claim to fame. 'This,' said Danny, 'is the biggest of the small lines.' Eh? 'There are three others with gauges of 15in or under: at Ravenglass, Bure Valley [in Norfolk] and Kirklees [near Huddersfield]. Ours goes on for 13.5 miles. We move 125,000 passengers a year, make a turnover of over £2 million and have 33 full-time staff, as well as 120 volunteers. We employ quite a few engineers all the year round, so we not only rebuild and maintain our own original engines and carriages, we also do a bit for other railways as well. In fact, we've just done some work for Ravenglass, because their workshop was burnt down about three years ago.'

These days, however, the Romney, Hythe and Dymchurch line was not entirely dependent on the tourist trade. Regular passengers included what you might call the shopping shareholders. 'They're mainly elderly people who buy shares in the railway and can then travel for free,' Danny explained. 'Most of them want to either go shopping in Hythe or travel down to our restaurant at Dungeness.

'For many years this line was used to take children to and from school. They'd travel from Dymchurch to New Romney where there's a big secondary school. It used to be the John Southland's Comprehensive, but now it's called the Marsh Academy. We'd have 110 kids on it at one time, but the numbers have dropped right down recently and the finances don't make sense any more. We stopped it last year.'

Our driver on the 11.15 to Dungeness had been one of those schoolkids. Zac Clark had been brought up in Dymchurch in a house backing on to the line, and had become involved with the railway from an early age. He'd qualified as a driver three months previously.

'This is my first full-time job,' he said proudly, giving the engine one more loving polish as departure time approached. Somewhat bafflingly for a railway in the far south of England, it or rather 'she' was called *Northern Chief*. Maybe that was because she had spent some time in the 1970s helping out up at Ravenglass in the Lake District. In fact, she had been one of Count Zborowski's first purchases, along with *Green Goddess*, and she'd pulled the first official train from Hythe to New Romney in August 1926, with the Duke of York on board.

Since she was no more than 5ft 4in high, I felt like patting her on the head, or at least the funnel. A daft idea, of course, because it was issuing steam and would have been boiling hot. No room for a fireman as well in that dinky cab, so the driver was something of a one-man band.

'What was it like, Zac, going to school on a train like this? A bit "parky" in the winter months, I should think.'

'It was all right,' he shrugged. 'Some liked it, some didn't.'

'Not like a school bus, though, was it?'

'That's what they all go on now. In my day there used to be 17 carriages packed with kids. Eventually it was down to two coaches and three kids. It couldn't go on.'

Well, at least there was a good turn-out of passengers today, some of them school age and some younger. Half way along the platform, a little girl was sobbing and stamping her foot. 'I want to go on *THAT* train,' she bawled, pointing at some stationary carriages nearby. Her father patiently pointed out that *THAT* train wasn't going anywhere, and eventually managed to lure her on to the 11.15 with minutes to go. I made sure that I found a carriage as far away as possible.

There was another small child in here. He came over and introduced himself. 'I'm Bradley,' he said, 'and I'm nearly three.'

'These small trains are ideal for him,' said his dad, Rob Fagg. Did that mean the lad had the splendid name of Bradley Fagg? Sounded like an actor from the 1930s who might have trodden the boards of provincial repertory theatres for years before making it big in the West End. Then again, his mother was Helen Bakeman, so it may be that he took her surname. I didn't like to ask.

'It's over 10 years since I was here,' Rob continued. 'Perhaps because I was a kid myself, it seemed much bigger then.' At least it didn't seem too cramped. The seats were comfortably padded and the sliding doors were open, allowing blasts of smoke to tickle the nostrils. The comparatively small scale of this railway, however, meant that we were low down and close to the rails. That, in turn, imparted a sense of speed that must have appealed to those racing drivers from the roaring twenties. In reality we were travelling at not much more than 20mph. Plenty of time to take in the passing sights, including cabbage whites fluttering around the abundant hanging baskets dangling from every platform lamp post. There were bloom-bedecked pots, too. At one point, not far out of Hythe, there was a little model of a man made entirely out of flowerpots. Somehow it reminded me of one of the children's puppet shows on the 12in black-and-white tellies of my own childhood. Was it Bill or was it Ben?

Rob or Helen wouldn't know, and neither would Bradley. His mouth had been agape since the moment we set forth. Perhaps he had already inherited the family love of railways – the Fagg family at least. 'My dad loved trains,' Rob was saying, 'and so did my grandad. He was a bus driver in London after the war, but he drove trains on this line in his spare time. Dad used to bring me down to travel on it and I was fascinated. He also knew the woman who ran one of the lighthouses at Dungeness, and I stayed the night there once. Didn't get much sleep.'

Well, I don't suppose you would if somebody kept switching the light on and off, I thought as we ran alongside a river shimmering in the morning sunlight. Soon we were out into open countryside, or rather marshland, with reeds running alongside the drainage dykes, crows swooping low over the heads of recumbent cows, and sheep grazing nearby, seemingly oblivious to occasional toots from *Northern Chief*. Romney Marsh lamb is sought after by gourmets because of its richness and its slight sweetness of flavour. Not too sweet, mind you. There's a natural salty edge because those were saltmarshes out there, peppered with samphire, as it were. No fertilisers, apparently, and perhaps because they're tucking into so much natural goodness, the sheep tend to produce extra fat which marbles the meat, adding to the flavour and making it moist. That's what it says on the Slow Food movement's website anyway and I don't doubt it, having once sampled the meat at a restaurant in Brighton. Memorable, to put it mildly.

We passed through several halts, stopping at some and sailing through others. As we pulled into Dymchurch Station, Helen asked: 'Do you want to get off and go to the beach, Bradley, or stay on the train?'

The answer came back emphatically: 'Stay on the train.' The same response was forthcoming when we finally reached Romney Sands. We'd already pulled in at New Romney, a sizeable station to be sure. It housed the engine sheds, an imposing signal box, a large cafe complete with model railway and an exhibition dedicated to this line's prominent role in World War II.

As if on cue a recently restored engine called *Winston Churchill* pulled in on the opposite line. Very impressive it looked, too, although I'm not sure how the arch-Conservative Prime Minister would have felt about being painted bright red.

I planned to call in at New Romney on the way back. For the time being, Dungeness beckoned. Quite a few new passengers had joined us by now, including a German family who told me they were on holiday, and a woman who countered the smell of smoke by tying a green handkerchief over her mouth and nose as though she were cycling in central London.

Soon we were leaving the marshland behind, and running alongside back-garden fences. And we were so low down that all you could see were the tops of sheds or greenhouses or washing lines. When the line had first been laid out, and for some time later, there would have been sea views all the way. Now all we had were occasional glimpses when we passed over open level crossings or, in one case, past a sizeable caravan park. But just when the journey seemed to be becoming a little tedious, suddenly there was shingle by the side of the line. The landscape began to open up.

And what a landscape! There was something other-worldly about it. Or at least 'other-England'. I'd been to most parts of this country, but I'd never clapped eyes on anything quite like this. To say it was flat would make it sound boring. But it wasn't. There was something vastly expansive about it. We may have been

The Observation Car Pluto *on the RHDR's 'Bluecoaster Express', which ran from 1947 to 1951*

Black Prince *at a rather bleak Dungeness in the late 1930s. The railway restaurant, recently extended and rebuilt, is noted for its locally caught fish and chips*

The RHDR as school train, taking children from Dymchurch to New Romney to the John Southland Comprehensive School in 1977

The armoured train, powered by no. 5 Hercules, *that ran on the RHDR during the last war, manned by soldiers of the Royal Engineers*

at the end of the line, the far end of England, but the plant-strewn shingle looked as though it might go on forever. The mountains of Wales and the Lake District, even the hills of the Cotswolds, Shropshire and the Malverns, might have been a million miles away. Put a four-lane highway across it with huge trucks and long cars, replace the shingle with cotton fields, and we could have been in the Deep South of America.

Thank goodness there was nothing like a four-lane highway at Dungeness. Even cars seemed few and far between. There was a nuclear power station, however, within a few hundred yards of the narrow-gauge railway station. Not to mention two lighthouses either side of the line. You wait all this time to see a lighthouse and two come along at once. Apparently they'd had no fewer than seven here at various times. The most recent had been built in 1961, and the whole tower was floodlit at night in order to reduce the bird mortality rate, Dungeness being something of a haven for our more unusual feathered friends. What is now called the Old Lighthouse was built in 1904 and opened by the then Prince of Wales. Today it was open to visitors with four quid to spare. Rob was evidently resigned to carrying Bradley up all 169 steps to the top.

I decided to leave them to it as I was feeling a bit peckish. The station's restaurant was rammed and there wasn't a table to be had, but I'd been told there was a pub called the Pilot that did fabulous fish and chips, albeit a little on the large side. But everyone I asked told me it was a 'fair old walk' and I wanted to see the famous Derek Jarman garden.

Luckily there was another pub, the Britannia, much closer to hand, or rather feet, which offered fish and chips too, including a 'small cod', which sounded just fine. And so it proved, especially when washed down with a pint of Shepherd Neame Master Brew. I sat on a bench outside enjoying a brisk breeze from the nearby sea and marvelling at the vastness of the skyscape. Great flocks of birds seemed to explode across it at regular intervals. I'd read on a nearby noticeboard that Dungeness was not only 'one of the largest areas of vegetative shingle in Europe', it was also 'a great place to find migratory birds'. Spiders, too. Not to mention greater crested newts and 'medicinal leeches'. And there was me thinking that letting leeches suck the blood had gone out of medical practice somewhere between Samuel Pepys's diary and Dickens's naughty nurse, Sairey Gamp.

Then again, until somebody mentioned it on the train I didn't know that Dungeness was Britain's only official desert. Still, at least there was water not too far away. Salt water, of course: hence all the fish on menus hereabouts. Just down the road from the Britannia, I stumbled across a hut selling crab, 'lobster rolls' and many other shelled or scaled delights. Would have been just what I'd have wanted had I not just seen off cod and chips.

The famous Jarman garden was a little further on. Derek Jarman was a film director, whose most famous work was probably *Caravaggio*, based on the Renaissance artist of the same name. His other films included *The Last of England*, based on one of his books. No, it wasn't about life at Dungeness.

Jarman died in 1994 but his garden lives on. It was designed from driftwood and plants found on the marsh. Don't ask me what they were. Let's just say that they looked suitably other-worldly. It was somewhat surprising to see protruding from the shingle what looked like a rusting wrench of the sort used to prise nuts off car wheels. Also washing on the line next door to this distinctive house of black wood with yellow window frames. There was a notice asking visitors to respect the privacy of the residents. 'Peering through the windows is particularly unwelcome.' Fair enough. I looked at the windows from a distance and noticed, even from there, that those yellow frames were badly in need of a lick of paint. Must be all those salty breezes coming in across flat shingle, sometimes turning into gales propelling horizontal rain.

Well, there must be some downsides to Dungeness. Certainly there was plenty more to see, including a bird observatory, the remains of one of Queen Victoria's personal railway carriages and, indeed, some rather more humble former Southern Region railway coaches that provided the basis for the homes of local fishermen. Also close to the coast on the other side of the shingle were what looked like great bowls of hollowed-out concrete. These, apparently, were known as the 'acoustic mirrors', and had been designed sometime between the two World Wars to pick up sound waves from invading aircraft.

There were plenty of trains back, so I got off at New Romney, where there was a good old-fashioned signal box with levers as well as computer-driven lights. Keeping an eye on both was 21-year-old Alex Ross, a weekend volunteer who worked as a technical officer on the main line back at Sittingbourne, where I'd recently been. 'I've been manning the signals here for two years,' he confided. 'Ultimately I want to be a driver, but you have to work your way up.'

It didn't seem to bother him that he'd been on duty since eight this morning and wouldn't leave until seven this evening. 'I love it here,' he said. 'Been coming since I was a toddler and my dad was doing some shifts. Most narrow-gauge lines have a single track with loops for passing trains. This one is double-tracked all the way back to Hythe.'

There was just time to pop into the museum of the 1940s, marking how 'the world's smallest public railway became part of the nation's war machine'. The bit about being 'the world's smallest' was presumably before it became 'the biggest of the small lines'. But there was no denying that 'the Kent coast was Britain's front line'. The Romney, Hythe and Dymchurch had been used to transport men and materials to Dungeness. Trains had to be armour-plated and camouflaged. 'Materials' included piping to move vital oil under the

Channel, and the parts to build another great acoustic ear as early warning of incoming aeroplanes had, with the Battle of Britain, become critical.

The museum incorporated a little cinema showing newsreels of what had been going on here, serenaded by what sounded like Joe Loss and his Orchestra. (My mum would have known, for sure.) There were also plenty of war-time posters and pictures of Churchill round the walls. Plus a photograph of the comedian Tommy Handley. He was standing on the footplate of the *Green Goddess* as she prepared to pull the *ITMA Special* to entertain the troops somewhere down the line.

It was now time to go down that final stretch of the line back to Hythe. 'Would you like a cockle, crab and jellied eel flavoured crisp?' somebody was asking his kids. They dug in.

'What flavour are they really?' I enquired.

'Salt and vinegar. I think we spent too much time in that fish hut in Dungeness,' he added before going on to tell me that he used to live in one of the houses backing on to the line. 'I would wave at these trains. Now I come back to ride on them twice a year. Mind you, we only live in Hythe.'

I was beginning to see the appeal of travelling on these little trains – not just for locals like this crisp-munching family from Hythe but for those who had come a considerable distance to take a correspondingly short journey. This was my third such expedition, and I was starting to take in how embedded these lines were in our history, whether they'd been set up to transport sand, the products of print works, or simply to satisfy the whims of wealthy men. And as for the scenery, that had already varied from wildflower meadows in Bedfordshire and views of the Chiltern Hills to the marshland beyond Sittingbourne and these extensive flatlands at the end of England.

Now I was off to North Wales, the heartland of Britain's narrow-gauge railways – a cornucopia of lines that I knew would take me up among steep and sweeping hills as well as up even steeper mountainsides: enough to ride a different one every day for a week.

Soon the desert of Dungeness would seem as far away as the dark side of the Moon.

4

A CLEAN SLATE

THE FFESTINIOG RAILWAY

Travelling on the Ffestiniog Railway to Blaenau Ffestiniog in a ffirst-class Pullman carriage on the ffinal train out of Porthmadog proved to be a ffine way to relax affter a ffraught Ffriday driving across the congested motorways of England and the bending by-ways of Wales where tractors trundle ffair distances between ffarmers' ffields.

OK, that's enough effing. And let me assure you that your correspondent is not normally a first-class travel sort of chap and I shall be in third class on the way back. I know my place. What's more, had I shelled out £22.60 for a return fare, I might not have been inclined to pay another seven quid each way for an upgrade. But when Andrew Thomas, former broadsheet journalist, volunteer track-layer and now head of the Ffestiniog's media relations, had dangled a pass to the Pullman in front of me, it was too tempting to resist. Anyway, the

The slate works at the Oakley Slate Quarry near Blaenau Ffestiniog, late 19th century

Ffestiniog markets itself as '150 years of first-class travel' – although I doubt it would have seemed too first-class back in the century before last if you'd had to ride one of those gravity slate trains from the quarries of Blaenau all the way down to the port at Porthmadog, which must have been terrifying.

'I've done it and it is,' Andrew confirmed.

'And working on the line?'

'That's wet, cold, miserable and splendidly refreshing if you've spent most of your working life in a warm office. And it's really nice when it stops.'

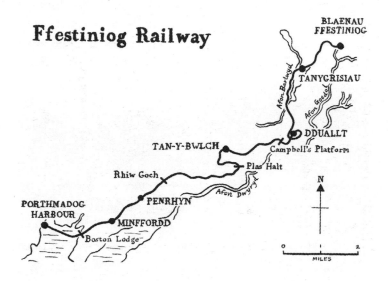

Ffestiniog Railway

So now at last I was riding this historic little railway: the one that had started all the others off, from Darjeeling to Romney Marsh. And these days, it had immediately become evident on my arrival at the Ffestiniog's Harbour Station, the Ffestiniog wasn't so little at all. With around 100 full-time employees, the railway was now the biggest employer in Porthmadog. Bigger even than the enormous branch of Tesco on the edge of town. But I quickly realised you could spot the volunteers: Welsh accents were less common among them than among the paid staff doing administrative jobs, working in the ticket office or serving in Spooner's Café-Bar and Grill.

Take the character I'd bumped into on the platform outside Spooner's. Mike Todd looked every inch the stationmaster. Not exactly the Fat Controller, but ample of girth and sporting a rather natty waistcoat under his uniform, complete with the sort of pocket watch and chain I'd always associated with aldermen in northern council chambers. Mike came originally from Yorkshire but, as he admitted, his accent had become somewhat 'blunted' by living in many another part of the country. 'I was a youth worker for years, but I was also a volunteer guard on these trains until I was 75.'

And how old was he now?

'Eighty,' he beamed through an impressive white beard. 'I suffer badly from gout, but I still like to come down here and see off a few trains. Mind you,' he stressed, 'I've never officially been a stationmaster.'

And if Mike might have stepped straight from the pages of *The Railway Children* or *Thomas the Tank Engine*, the guard on our train that *Iarll Meirionnydd* (Earl of Merioneth) was about to haul on the winding, continuously uphill route to Blaenau wouldn't have sounded out of place among commuters on the 8.25 from Surbiton to Waterloo. As for the driver, Alex Crooks, he came from Leicester. 'I'm an electrical engineer by trade,' he told me as he hurried past on his way to take command of the 15.45. 'I just really enjoy doing this at weekends. It's so different round here.' Very different from Leicester, that's for sure.

The first-class Pullman was the last carriage on our train. The curved windows at the back offered a panoramic view. The seats were tall and wing-backed. They reminded me of the Parker Knoll armchairs you find in old people's homes and sometimes advertised in the Weekend section of the *Telegraph*.

Very comfortable, needless to say. I was reclining in mine, taking in the etched-glass panelling and the highly polished wooden tables, when a couple climbed aboard at the last minute. He was munching Maltesers; she was taking the first bite from a Snickers Bar. 'He's in our seat,' she said in a strong Yorkshire accent, slightly muffled by chocolate.

'He is,' her husband confirmed.

Although slightly baffled by being referred to in the third person, I stood up immediately and offered to move. 'No, he's all right,' said Snickers-woman.

'Ay, he is,' said he, leading the way to an adjoining table where he began to bend her ear with a detailed description of a journey he had made on the Scarborough to Pickering line, seemingly oblivious to the beauty that began to unfold beyond the window almost as soon as we had pulled out of Porthmadog. The sun was gleaming on the Glaslyn Estuary as we passed over the Cob causeway, built between 1807 and 1811 to reclaim land from the sea, and chuffed and chugged and hissed and hooted onwards and upwards at 20mph.

One of a party of young-ish couples who had bagged the tables with the panoramic view had left

Princess *at Harbour Station, 1871*

Palmerston *at Minffordd, 1870s (note the headless driver)*

his glass of Prosecco, picked up his expensive-looking camera and was now leaning out of one of the windows. Above his head was a sign warning passengers about the dangers of sticking your head out – a legacy, perhaps, of the days when all trains had pull-down windows on the doors and there was always the possibility of being decapitated by the *Flying Scotsman* or some other express hurtling past in the opposite direction.

In truth, there didn't appear to be much of a risk on this single-track line. The first crossing point was at Minffordd, where we were afforded a sighting of *Dafydd Lloyd George*, better known to some of us as David, chugging downhill and passing by on a loop. Like the Earl (or *Iarll*) pulling us, it was built comparatively recently and completed in 1992 at the hugely impressive Boston Lodge engine works we had passed not long after leaving the Cob. No less an authority than the *Guinness Book of Records* has recognised it as the oldest works in the world, building locomotives in the 19th, 20th and 21st centuries. Restoring them, too. Thanks to the work done here, *Merddin Emrys* is still running up and down the line as it has done, on and off, since 1879. It's one of the Double Fairlies, for those of you who like to know about these things, designed by the great Robert Francis Fairlie. It was to him that the line's secretary and manager, George Easton Spooner, had turned after previously employing George England, whose locomotives had proved not quite up to the task of pulling heavier loads as the slate trade boomed. England was not happy. Apart from anything else, he had brought a court case against Fairlie a few years earlier – for eloping to Spain and marrying his daughter when she was still of an age to require her father's permission. Unfortunately for England, it came out during the trial that he himself had eloped with his daughter's mother. And he already had a wife who was still alive at the time! Case dismissed. Fairlie was found not guilty.

Now here he was in 1870, unveiling in front of engineers from around the world what looked like two engines back to back. In fact, it appears to have been *Princess*, designed by England seven years previously, that became the first narrow-gauge steam loco to pull trucks here on the Ffestiniog. Also built in 1863 and pulling its first passenger train two years later, *Princess*'s sibling, *Prince*, was overhauled at Boston Lodge for its 150th birthday, and the old boy was still making occasional stately appearances, it seemed, notably helping to pull the Santa Special.

As we'd pulled out across the Cob, the harbour beyond the station car park at Porthmadog had looked more like a marina than a port. Leisure craft bobbed in the peaceful waters. It was hard to imagine this had once been the 'Tyneside of Wales'. At its peak, over a thousand ships a year were there to take slate freight from the nearby station on its onward journey. Some 116,000 tons of the stuff were shipped all over the world. Crane chains would be clanging and stevedores bawling. And now? Apart from the cry of gulls and a few residents enjoying a late-afternoon drink on the balconies of surrounding apartments, all you could hear was the rattle of ropes on masts in a light breeze.

So what happened to that slate freight?

Well, by the early 1900s piles of the stuff were gathering dust on the quayside at Porthmadog and elsewhere. The export trade had declined markedly since the 1880s, partly because of the imposition of duties on foreign slate by countries such as France and Switzerland. But it was the downturn of sales to Germany that hit the Ffestiniog area particularly badly. And still to come was a World War, fairly closely followed by another. Oh, yes, and in between was the small matter of the economic depression of the 1920s and 1930s. Not to mention the development of roofing tiles, used more and more by the building industry from the mid-1920s onwards. Then the English Board of Education began discouraging the use of chalking on slate in schools – for the children, if not the teachers. It could be said that the writing was on the wall for the industry and the narrow-gauge railways that had served it so well. Then came World War II.

From 1865 onwards, the Ffestiniog line had always transported passengers as well as freight – intrepid travellers, you might well call them, in the early days. The outbreak of hostilities in 1939, however, put an end to that source of revenue as well. No wonder there were so few railway staff remaining by the end of the war. On 2 August 1946, the general manager sent them a letter. There's a copy of it in the Gwynedd Archives at Caernarfon. Addressed to a Mr T J Roberts of Tunnel Cottage, near Blaenau Ffestiniog, it read:

'Dear Sir,

There will be no further traffic conveyed over this Railway and the service of the staff is dispensed with. I therefore regret having to inform you that your services will not be required after tomorrow the 3rd instant.

Yours faithfully,

Robert Evans'

Not surprisingly, the rolling stock, the line and the buildings that had served it so well deteriorated rapidly. John Winton described it graphically in the prologue to the 1975 edition of his book *The Little Wonder, 150 years of the Festiniog Railway*.

'The wagons and rails in the marshalling yard at Minffordd were covered in a thick, thorny carpet of brambles waving like prairie grass in the wind... Weeds ran riot on the permanent way. Trees grew

from shoots to saplings as big as a man's leg. Drains
and ditches were blocked up. After heavy rain, rushing
streams carried away stretches of the track… Wooden
fencing and boards rotted away. Walls crumbled.
Cuttings became water-filled. Water poured
constantly from the hillside into the Long Tunnel.
Sleepers and keys were stolen for firewood. The line
was taken over by sheep…'

Who on earth would want to buy such a line?

Someone with more money than sense, perhaps.
Someone who was a railway enthusiast imbued with
that can-do attitude that grew out of the wreckage of
war. That someone was Alan Pegler, who acquired the
railway in 1954 and started recruiting the first team of
volunteers to begin the lengthy and formidable process
of clearing and rebuilding.

Alan Pegler was a corpulent and be-whiskered
figure – 'a jovial, extrovert character of Falstaffian
proportions', as the *Telegraph* put it his obituary when
Pegler finally pegged it in 2012. He was 91 and had
been married four times. A full life, you might well
say. A Cambridge graduate and an old boy of
Radley School, after rescuing the Ffestiniog Pegler
rescued the *Flying Scotsman* from going to the
scrapyard and then managed to lose the family fortune
taking her to America. Having been born in a posh
part of London, he finished up renting a flat over a fish
and chip shop opposite Paddington Station. 'Handy for
train watching,' he shrugged. Then he set about freeing

himself from bankruptcy by impersonating Henry VIII at the Tower of London and working as a host-guide on the *Orient Express*. And throughout much of that long life, he kept returning to Wales to oversee and encourage the Herculean efforts of those volunteers.

The first, short section, from Porthmadog to Boston Lodge, reopened in 1955. Alan Heywood remembered it well. He was a young shaver of 15 at the time, living in Bury in Lancashire, and that was the first summer that he travelled down here. 'I came with some of the lads from the railway club at school,' he'd told me over a cup of tea in Spooner's at Harbour Station, shortly before I'd set off on the 15.45 to Blaenau. 'They'd cleared the first mile of track, but there was still grass halfway up the sides of the carriages. Beyond Boston Lodge it was totally overgrown by trees. Obviously I had an interest in railways, and here was an opportunity to *do* something rather than just watch trains from the side of the line. My first job was to climb on the roof of a carriage and slap on some Bitumastic to seal up the holes.'

'Was it exciting just being here in those days?'

'Oh, yes. And you had a feeling that you were involved in something pioneering. It was more than that, though. It was the ability to get involved and to feel as though you were doing a real man's job.'

Alan went to university in Swansea, a damn sight nearer than Bury, and continued to work on the railway during the long summer vacations. 'I trained as a

guard, worked here seven days a week and met all sorts
of people. There were locals, some of whom told me
that they used to go to school on this train, but there
were many more holidaymakers. Some of them were
baffled by the narrow-gauge element of the line. They
couldn't understand how some of the trains could go,
because they couldn't see the wheels. In those days,
remember, most people went on holiday to the seaside
for a fortnight.'

Ah, yes, I remember it well. And while rural and
coastal Wales was – and is – stunningly beautiful for the
most part, it can't guarantee the weather to lie on the
beach all day. Taking a trip on the railway was
'something to do,' as Alan put it. He should know,
having watched the line extend, the number of visitors
grow to over 200,000 a year and the once run-down
town of Porthmadog prosper and transform itself as a
result. Having worked as a teacher in his native
Lancashire, he'd moved down here with his wife
permanently in 1969. 'My job was operating the
commercial side as traffic manager,' he said. 'It didn't
pay as well as teaching, but it was a chance to make a
living out of my hobby.'

As I'd driven west earlier in the day, the voluptuous
hills of Shropshire and Herefordshire had looked
particularly ravishing. But once you're over the Welsh
border, the hills immediately become steeper and
greener. You start asking yourself: how did that sheep
get all the way up there, and how is it managing to stay

upright when it appears to be at 90 degrees to the ground? Ensconced in our first-class carriage in high summer, we were passing through some of the most spectacular scenery in Britain. Waterfalls cascaded and streams frothed down mossy rock-sides. Mountainous swathes of deep green grass soared on one side while valleys dipped away spectacularly on the other, affording the chance to look down on treetops far below us. Sheep were everywhere – clinging to improbably steep crags, lurking on golden bracken and, in one or two cases, a few feet from the line. Having somehow penetrated the fence alongside, they looked terrified as a green monster steamed past, breathing smoke and flexing powerful pistons. Sharp bends in the line offered those of us entranced rather than terrified splendid views of the engine through much closer trees in full bloom. I was up here in North Wales to travel on five narrow-gauge lines in five days and, by the end, I would feel as though I had gorged on a glut of glorious countryside.

Occasionally there would appear reminders of more mundane life carrying on in the real world – some poor sods waiting patiently for a rural bus to appear, a line of washing hanging limply in the garden of a comparatively humble cottage. It had a slate roof, like every other building in these parts. There was slate on the roofs of the immaculately painted shelter in every halt we pulled into. Slate on the original locomotive shed we had passed earlier in the journey, built in 1963 and handsomely restored in 2009. Slate on the nearby Plas Penrhyn on the hillside just above Boston Lodge.

According to my guidebook, this house 'with its beautiful ornate veranda offering views towards the Llyn [peninsula] and Snowdon' was once the home of Samuel Holland, MP for Merioneth and one of the first promoters helping to bring in the capital to build the Ffestiniog Railway. His cousin, the Victorian novelist Elizabeth Gaskell, was a frequent visitor. Later the house became home to Bertrand Russell, philosopher, mathematician, winner of the Nobel Prize for Literature and renowned political campaigner.

Whether he ever involved himself in campaigns to improve the working lives of slate miners is not recorded. One thing's for sure: those men lived dangerously. If huge slabs of slate tumbling unexpectedly from the high roofs of the quarries didn't flatten them, their lungs would be infected by inhaling lethal dust and they would wheezily deteriorate while suffering from silicosis. The graveyard we had just passed was apparently full of former slate miners, quarrymen, call them what you will. The average age of those buried there was 32.

A sobering thought, for sure, and one that was only interrupted by the arrival of a fresh-faced young volunteer called Ben offering the drinks menu. More Prosecco for those in the window seat. And for me? A Welsh Gold, thank you very much. The selection of 'craft' or 'artisan' beers available on the Ffestiniog made

3594 *Ffestiniog* *Double Engine*

James Spooner, *one of the Ffestiniog's original Double Fairlie locos, at Porthmadog*

Another slate works at Minffordd next to the Ffestiniog Railway

a pleasant change from the cans of fizzy lager or flavourless ales available from most mainline buffet bars or trolley services. 'Cheers,' I said to Ben just as an evangelical chapel came into view on the right-hand side. Such was the power of the Chapel not so long ago that pubs were closed on a Sunday in certain Welsh counties. Well, sorry, Minister, but the Sabbath was two days away and it was rapidly approaching that time on a Friday when I might set off for my local and an early-doors pint.

On this particular Friday, however, we were heading for the very different surroundings of Blaenau Ffestiniog. Towards the top of the line, the scenery began to change. Less green, more grey. The craggy outcrops of rock were man-made. These were spoil tips on mountains that looked as though they had been turned inside-out. The poet W H Auden was always fascinated by landscapes that had been man-made through industry or mining. His imagination seems to have been fired, according to Humphrey Carpenter's biography of him, by a boyhood visit to North Wales at Easter, 1914 on a family holiday, during which he saw the Ffestiniog's slate trains rolling down to the sea. From then on, narrow-gauge railways were an essential part of his favourite landscapes – those he defined pertinently in the title of one poem as 'Not in Baedeker'.

By the time Alan Heywood had moved down to North Wales for good, the Ffestiniog volunteers' back-breaking efforts had already reopened the line from

Porthmadog as far as Dduallt, a tiny halt on the hillside with no road access about two-thirds of the way back to Blaenau Ffestiniog. But it wasn't until 1982 that the first Ffestiniog train on the revived line had steamed into Blaenau. In the meantime, the Central Electricity Generating Board had flooded the valley below the next station up the line, Tan-y-Grisau, to create a pump storage scheme to generate electricity. As a result, the Ffestiniog's original 1836 route to its northern terminus was severed.

The court case of *Festiniog v Electricity Authority* went on for some 15 years. It wasn't until 1971 that the court found in favour of the railway and awarded it over £100,000 in compensation – enough money to build a new route to Blaenau.

To get there had required one of the most remarkable civil engineering projects ever undertaken by not only a narrow-gauge railway, but also a largely volunteer one. To get round the CEGB's reservoir the Ffestiniog had had to build the Deviation: a new route that required blasting a new tunnel. And to gain the height between the top of its old track and the bottom of its new track had required a great big spiral of track running across a new viaduct – while still maintaining the continuous downward incline that had enabled gravity to trundle a line of slate wagons all the way from Blaenau down to the sea.

In 1995 Alan Heywood had become general manager. By then the Ffestiniog had become involved in an even vaster project: to reopen the entire Welsh Highland Railway, another moribund narrow-gauge line, almost twice the length of the whole Ffestiniog, that had run from Porthmadog across Snowdonia towards the Caernarfon coast. They'd obviously pulled it off, as I had my ticket booked for the Welsh Highland later in the week, but that was another story. Alan, meanwhile, had become more and more involved with another offshoot of the Ffestiniog empire called Ffestiniog Travel. It had started out as a way of booking a few British Rail tickets for some Dutch enthusiasts who wanted to visit the line, and had developed into a substantial travel agency offering railway holidays riding on far-flung lines from Montenegro to Peru. Alan was still managing director at the age of 75.

I'd been in Blaenau Ffestiniog rather more recently than W H Auden, by which time Ffestiniog had acquired another 'f' and Porthmadog an 'h', while changing its 'c' for a 'g'. I'd been researching a book on Britain's lost mines. 'A lot of muscle and tears produced that landscape,' I remember being told by former lead-mine blacksmith Tom Roughead as we gazed at the slagheaps on the Crimea Pass, otherwise known as the A470.

'That part was known as the Quarry of Death,' he went on, waving a finger towards another grey crag beneath which was an underground chamber – one of many at the Oakley mine where he had worked. 'This one had clay beneath the veins and, when it dried out, things started moving. Any loud noise could bring a slab of slate crashing down.'

Bear in mind that there were not only miners who had to blast and hack their way through the headings or shafts to provide access to the slate. There were also 'rock men' who worked in pairs. The one at the top could be suspended 120ft in the air, abseiling across the roof of one of the many chambers, having climbed up there on much extended ladders. The one at the bottom had to ensure that the slab that came hurtling down had a cushioned landing on soft clay before he set about chipping it into shape without chopping it into pieces. And all the time he had to keep an eye out for those loose slabs that might come down on him like a ton of slate.

Tom had had an early taste of the hazards of mining when, aged 16, he was called upon to retrieve the missing arm of a man who had strayed too close to one of the belts in the mill. Four years later he had found himself peering into a tunnel where a miner had been trapped by falling slate. His leg had been crushed. 'The old doctor who turned up was too fat. "You're the thinnest," he said to me. "You crawl in and give him this injection." I did, and thank God he went out like a light.'

The X-ray department opposite the cosy home that Tom shared with his partner Ruth confirmed the scale of silicosis among slate miners after the National Health Service came into being in 1948. But as long ago as

1893 a government enquiry had found that the annual death rate for underground slate workers was 3.23 per thousand – higher than the rate for coal miners, and that was high enough. Muscle and tears, indeed. That extraordinary landscape was testament to both. As indeed was the graveyard that we had passed on the way here.

Oakley was one of the so-called 'big three' mines in Blaenau. There was also Votty, which was shut down in 1963, and Llechwedd, now reopened as a visitor attraction where you can still go on tours to find out the dark history that lies deep beneath the mountains of Snowdonia. The £20 entrance fee for the tour of Llechwedd's slate caverns involves another railway – a miniature one that takes you down some 500ft at a stately 5 miles per hour. What a day that could be: a narrow-gauge journey on the Ffestiniog through some of the most stunning scenery in the UK, followed by another ride into the bowels of the earth. So much more civilised than the days when miners put their limbs, lungs and lives on the line to get at the slate, and railway men sat precariously on top of it as it rolled down the line to the port.

After that eye-opening afternoon with the redoubtable Roughead I'd booked into a B&B that had turned out to be run by a woman and her son who sounded like characters from *EastEnders*. 'We're really from Essex,' she'd confided before asking if I'd be wanting a full Welsh breakfast in the morning. With lava bread.

It's fair to say that the shiny slate roofs of Blaenau do not have many eating and drinking places lurking beneath them. No matter. All I wanted was a pub where I could write up my notes and transcribe the interviews on my voice recorder. Preferably a pub with a curry house next door. And that's exactly what I'd found on the main street. Well-kept pint of Shepherd Neame Spitfire, too, even if it had been brewed some distance away in Faversham, Kent.

It didn't particularly bother me that everyone in the bar was speaking Welsh. I've always nurtured a secret admiration for those on the western side of Offa's Dyke who've made themselves completely bi-lingual. And that's only part of a cultural dimension that's very different from England. As we'd looked out over that distinctive landscape of inside-out mountains a few hours earlier, Tom Roughead had told me about the cultural side of slate mining. During their lunchtimes, or 'snap breaks', the miners would gather in the *caban* (cabin) for wide-ranging discussions on issues such as religion, education and politics. What's more, someone would be delegated to take formal minutes. There were also mini-Eisteddfods between different chambers of the mine. Choirs, brass bands and even poets would compete for a cup made out of an old syrup tin by Tom and his fellow blacksmith. I remember reflecting at the time that it's not just the scenery that makes North Wales distinctive from the rest of the UK.

And anyway, the barman was perfectly civil when I ordered another pint of Spitfire in English, having been out to peer through the window of the curry house to confirm that there was still not another soul inside, apart from a waiter or two. Maybe it would fill up later. Or maybe not, I thought, as hunger began to kick in and I glanced again across the pub at a table of middle-aged ladies who had been nattering away in Welsh. One of them had just returned from the fish and chip shop across the way with several bags of chips. They all dug in, including the landlady, who had been holding court for much of the evening.

It was time to be bold, I told myself. I sidled over. 'Can I do that?' I asked her. 'Bring in fish and chips, I mean.'

'Course you can, darling,' she beamed between mouthfuls.

The battered haddock went down very well with the Shepherd Neame and, having finished writing up my notes, I spent three-quarters of an hour or so chatting amicably to the local plumber, who happily switched to English for my benefit.

Not that I was planning another night out in Blaenau.

I joined my fellow passengers as we clambered aboard the 17.20 for the last train back that day. Not wishing to hear any more about the Scarborough–Pickering line, I chose to travel 'Third Class', which was nothing of the sort. The seats were perfectly well padded, if not as lavishly so as the Parker Knolls, and it didn't feel overcrowded or cramped. Everybody seemed to be eating, mind you, either sandwiches from pre-packed picnics or those bought from the station or on-board buffets. Ben made a re-appearance but, aware that I would eventually have to drive a short distance to my B&B, I reluctantly turned down his offer of another Welsh Gold.

Instead I revelled in the gold that seemed to be everywhere on the downhill return journey – filtering through the leaves, spilling on to the mirrored surface of rivers, reservoirs and lakes. The estuary was tinged with gold, too, as gulls swooped over the adjoining marshland and the sun began its steady descent towards the far west.

5

A TRAIN UP
A MOUNTAIN

The Snowdon Mountain Railway

It was a cloudy Sunday morning in Llanberis, and I seemed to be one of the few people without a stick. The old boy in the bungalow was carrying one, but then he'd just popped out to pick up a newspaper. Others clutched much longer sticks – the sort wielded by walkers with knapsacks on their backs and hiking boots encasing their ankles. Heaven knows, there were more than enough steep hills around here offering… well, heavenly views. But the best view of all was from the highest peak.

I'd come 25 miles from Porthmadog northeast to the heart of Snowdonia, one of the most magnificently mountainous regions on this island. Its principal peak, Snowdon, rises majestically to 1,085m, or 3,560ft in real money. It's not only the highest mountain in Wales, but the second-highest in Britain. Only Ben Nevis is *!!*

What?
56 mountains in
Scotland are higher than
Snowdon !

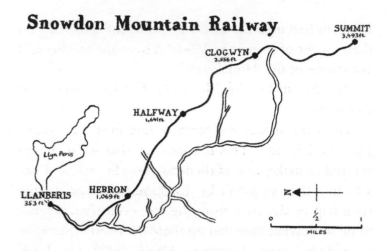

Snowdon Mountain Railway

SUMMIT
3,493 ft.

CLOGWYN
2,556 ft.

HALFWAY
1,641 ft.

Llyn Peris

LLANBERIS
353 ft.

HEBRON
1,069 ft.

N

0   ½   1
MILES

higher. And here, at the little town of Llanberis, I was
about to catch a train – Britain's only train up a
mountain – to the very top.

At a price, mind you. 'This'll be my first and last
trip,' muttered a bloke from Chester. 'It's just cost me
29 quid for a return.'

The queue waiting to board the 10.30 on the
Snowdon Mountain Railway to the summit was
surprisingly multi-cultural. I say 'surprisingly' because
my fellow travellers around narrow-gauge lines so far
had been predominantly white English. Here was a
potential train of many tongues: Punjabi as well as
Welsh and Japanese. Plus English, of course, and maybe
Tibetan too? I wasn't sure what language they were
talking but, in appearance at least, one of those small
groupings present could have been Himalayan. Perhaps
that was because, I'd been told, Sir Edmund Hillary and

his team had used the slopes of Snowdonia to train for their ascent of Everest in 1953. 'Where are you from?' I asked one of the 'Himalayans'.

'We live in London,' he said, effortlessly switching to English.

The same answer was forthcoming from a couple of Japanese heritage. 'This is a journey that we've always wanted to make,' one of them told me. Somehow I had a feeling they wouldn't be disappointed, either by the train trip or the view from the top, even if turned out to be somewhat crowded up there. I'd been chatting to the railway's general manager, Alan Kendall, who'd told me that 'Snowdon is probably the busiest mountain there is', with 130,000 to 150,000 passengers between May and October, 'and around 400,000 walkers as well'. One of the daft questions he'd been asked by a passenger about to set forth was 'Is there a branch of Marks and Spencer's up there?'

Daft insofar as getting planning permission to build a chain store on the summit of Snowdon would be about as likely claiming the right to herd sheep along Oxford Street. But not daft insofar as there would be more than enough potential customers. Particularly on Sunday mornings, if this one was anything to go by.

We of several tongues clambered aboard a single carriage with an incomprehensible name that translated as 'Welsh Mountain Goat'. The engine pushing us was called *Wyddfa*, otherwise known as Wilfred. That's what the Reverend Awdry, author of *Thomas the Tank*

Engine, called him as a stalwart of his stories of the Culdee Fell Railway. His story of *Mountain Engines* first appeared in 1964, the year after the writing Rev had visited the Snowdon line. It also featured an engine called *Ernest*, which appeared to have had a change of gender as well as name. *Ernest* was based on *Enid*, another veteran on this line. We had a glimpse of her as she passed us at the Clogwyn loop on her way down the mountain.

Enid and *Wyddfa* emerged from the Swiss Locomotive Works in Winterthur, Switzerland, and were built to last. By the time the railway celebrated its 120th anniversary in 2016, somebody calculated that *Enid* had covered a distance of 3,075,200km (getting on for 2 million miles). That's the equivalent of four journeys to the Moon and back. Bear in mind that the distance from Llanberis to the mountain top is only 4.7 miles (7.6km), albeit at an average gradient of 1 in 7.8 (1 in 5.5 at its steepest). Bear in mind also that the extraordinary mileage clocked up by these two railway workhorses was not just down to meticulous Swiss engineering. It also owed something to the maintenance administered at the engine sheds in Llanberis.

Unlike the Ffestiniog, the Snowdon Mountain Railway is entirely run by professionals. The 40 or so full-time staff spend the months between the end of October and beginning of May ensuring that the engines and rolling stock are kept in prime condition.

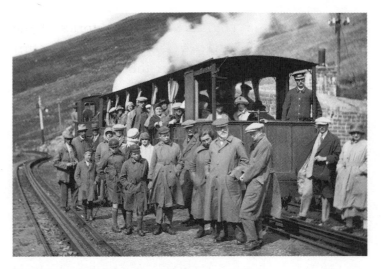

Passengers disembark on the way up Snowdon in a pre-war scene

*Passengers wait for a train back down the mountain at the old and far-from-picturesque
Summit Station*

Not only the steam engines but also the diesels, which arrived in the 1980s. Then there are the carriages. There was a *Snowdon Lily* as well as a *Mountain Goat*. *Lily* was rebuilt on the chassis of one of the originals imported by the Snowdon Mountain Tramroad and Hotels Co. Ltd in 1896.

The fascinating history of how a Swiss rack-and-pinion railway came to be built up a Welsh mountain is a subject to which we shall return. So what about the journey from Llanberis to Yr Wydffa Station at the top? We'd be setting off any minute now. Promise. Before we did I just wanted to grab a quick word with our driver.

Robert Jones was fairly typical of the Snowdon line employees insofar as he followed in his father's footsteps. 'Dad worked here from 1970 to 1990, and that's when I took over, which means that I've driven here even longer than he did,' Robert reflected. 'I'm 45 now, and this is basically all I've known. It's what I grew up with, as Dad sometimes let me ride with him, though I never take it for granted. It's still very special.'

Not that he had much chance to take in the scenery once he was in the cab. On this line, the engine pushed rather than pulled. Robert could see through the wide windows of the single carriage ahead of him, but not closely enough to spot a broken rail or an obstruction on the line – sheep, for the most part. His guiding eyes today were provided by Amanda Ward, the guard, standing at the front of the carriage and ready to raise her arm as a signal to stop if necessary. Amanda's father also worked on the Snowdon Mountain, while her grandfather was a guard on the main line. 'I've still got his whistle,' she showed me on the way down when she could relax and enjoy the views that she, too, never seemed to tire of.

One of the first things I noticed on the way up, as the rooftops and treetops quickly shrank away beneath us, was another spectacular waterfall cascading down a steep rock-face into the gorge below. 'You should see it after it's been raining,' somebody said. I was still trying to take in the sheer numbers of walkers climbing the craggy landscape alongside us every step of the way, as though embarking on a pilgrimage. Some were waving cheerfully, others keeping an eye out for their children or trying to restrain their dogs from chasing sheep. A few 'walkers' were even running. 'That's showing off,' grinned Jeff Lawrence, a retired policeman from Kent who used to ride on the Romney, Hythe and Dymchurch line to deter yobs from throwing stones at the trains. 'There aren't too many mountains there. That's why we've come to Snowdon. For a change,' he added, before introducing me to his wife Jo and 10-year-old daughter Emma.

'All the same,' I suggested to Jeff, 'if you've worked on a railway for a while, this must seem a bit like a busman's holiday. What's so special about narrow-gauge lines?'

'I think there's a romantic feel about them – a sense of going back in time, with the smell of smoke and the sight of steam. I also like the enthusiasm of the volunteers on so many of these lines, and the way that the trains go through scenery that I haven't seen before.'

Not for the first time I found myself contemplating the extraordinary contrasts in landscape within a couple of hundred miles or so. Certainly it's difficult to imagine more of a contrast than between the flat, wide-open shingle of Dungeness at the end of the Romney, Hythe and Dymchurch line on the far southeastern edge of England, and the mountainside of Snowdon as it thrust through the clouds towards the highest point in Wales. Small island, different world.

Once we had left behind the gorge, the two viaducts above it and the remnants of an ancient oak forest, we emerged into open, treeless countryside and caught the first glimpse of the sharp peak of Snowdon poking above the right-hand side of the ridge ahead of the train.

Down here on the lower slopes were some small-scale ruined buildings that were little more than piles of stone. Former shepherds' huts, perhaps? No, this was once a community of over a hundred people. The men earned a living, of sorts, in the slate quarries of Dinorwig. They supplemented their meagre earnings by raising animals and harvesting hay. Somehow, I learnt from Amanda later, they scraped together enough money to build themselves a chapel. By the end of the

1950s the community had all gone, apparently, but the chapel building was still there in 1966 when it was bought by a man from Birmingham for £450. Over 50 years on and there's not much of it left. Its name lives on, however, in the station called Hebron. Incidentally, it wasn't just slate that came out of the steep slopes hereabouts. There was also a copper mine at Clogwyn Goch, and another in the black volcanic rock further up the line.

Higher up the mountain, too, was a potential treat for twitchers. As the train emerged from a cutting, we could see across to the Hill of the Falcon, one of many Snowdonian homes for the peregrine falcon. To its north, I'd read, lay a cave from which it is believed that Owain Glyndwr led the last rebellion against the English. Shakespeare called him Owen Glendower in *Henry IV* Part One, and had the fiery Hotspur imply that he was the original Welsh windbag. Scurrilous English nonsense, no doubt.

We stopped at Halfway Station to take on some much-needed water – for the engine, that is. On the far side of the valley lay Moel Cynghorion, the Mountain of the Councillors, where the Welsh princes held their councils during the reign of Edward I.

Duly watered, we pushed on, or rather up. The gradient seemed to be getting steeper all the time. Clogwyn Station, on the loop where *Enid* passed us on the way down, offered a view of the sheer rock face of Clogwyn du't Arddu, otherwise known as 'Cloggy',

Assorted Snowdon Mountain Railway tickets

where Hillary used to go climbing. That's Sir Edmund Hillary to you and me. It was on those vertical rocks, often covered in ice during the winter, that he and his fellow adventurers had trained for the first successful ascent of Everest.

They would have worn helmets, carefully strapped under the chin. Not so the intrepid train travellers who ventured on to this line when it was in its infancy. They wore hats, as almost everyone did on social occasions in the 19th and early 20th centuries. Toppers and bowlers for the men, perhaps, and something a little more elegantly broad-brimmed for the ladies. Not a good idea at this gradient when the carriages were still open-topped. Off they flew like frisbees when the passengers stood up to look down on to the Llanberis Pass, or the Valley of the Hats as it's known today. To dwellers in the hamlet of Nant Peris that headgear was like manna from on high. 'There must have been some pretty fancy hats in the chapel there every Sunday,' Amanda speculated.

Certainly the residents hereabouts would have had little spare cash for hats in those days. They scraped a living from the land or the mines and quarries beneath. A little further up, where the line was at its steepest, was a chance not only to marvel at the view all the way back down to Llanberis, but also to take in the scale of the Dinorwig Quarry. Back in the early 1880s, the quarries round here were the second largest in Wales. Nearly 3,000 men and boys prised 90,000 tons of slate from the mountainside each year. Some small slabs were used to mark their early graves.

Suddenly the track was levelling out, and we were easing to a halt. This was as far as you could go. I pushed my way through the comparatively new, expanded but extremely busy visitor centre and joined the crowd surging towards the summit. There were so many of us that I shouldn't have been surprised to find a *Big Issue* seller up there.

It was a few degrees colder than it had been at what you might call base camp. But that's not always the case. 'The weather is one thing you can't predict about Snowdon,' Alan Kendall had told me. One half-term was so hot at the top, apparently, that Amanda had found herself giving water to the passengers. 'The rest of the country was wet and cold, but it was 30 degrees up here. What's more, it was really clear. You could see the whole of the coast of Ireland, and the Isle of Man.'

And the view, when I clambered up a very well-worn path and found myself among a scrum of selfie-takers at the very top of Snowdon?

Well, the higher you go in Wales the more you begin to run out of the oxygen of superlatives. Below me was one of the world's most breathtaking panoramas. Although we were looking down on the clouds, it wasn't *that* clear today. You couldn't see much of Anglesey, let alone the coast of Ireland. What I could see much closer to us were some Alpine flowers and lots of ferns. 'Very rare ferns, they are,' said somebody squeezed in next to me. At which point my contemplation of this fabled volcanic landscape was interrupted by a group of young men with bulky knapsacks on their backs, running up the path and into our midst. 'We did that all the way from the bottom of the mountain,' one of them assured me. 'Running, I mean.' He didn't even sound too breathless, and the accompanying wink confirmed that his claim was not exactly serious.

There was a gold-topped stone at the summit's centre on which were engraved directions to various landmarks, including the University of Wales's campus at Bangor. By now, though, the knapsacks were making it even more congested up here, so I retreated back down the path, still contemplating that it was somewhere up here that the Welsh princes had held council for centuries. They had looked down, literally and no doubt metaphorically, on those tiny communities of farmers and miners.

Unlike many a narrow-gauge line in Wales, however, the transportation of slate was not the prime purpose behind the formation of the Snowdon Mountain Railway. The top of that mountain might have seemed halfway to the stars for those peering up it from Llanberis exactly a hundred years before mankind made the giant leap to land on the Moon. It seems appropriate in the circumstances that it was a certain Sir Richard Moon who in 1869 proposed laying a line to the summit. Moon was the chairman of the London and North Western Railway, and a branch line from Bangor to Llanberis had been completed in that year. Why not carry on onwards and upwards, offering the burgeoning Victorian tourist market a chance to revel in those sublime views?

One reason was the local landowner, one George William Duff Assheton-Smith, whose list of objections was even longer than his name. Initial Parliamentary Bills were met with stiff opposition, and an acrimonious debate broke out in the letters column of *The Times*. Another fierce opponent of the proposed line was Canon Hardwick D Rawnsley, secretary of the newly formed National Trust.

The deadlock was finally broken after the opening of the narrow-gauge Welsh Highland Railway to Rhyd Ddu on the mountain's southwest flank in 1881, leading to a significant loss of trade in Llanberis. Even worse, the terminus of that railway was renamed Snowdon, thereby attracting tourists away from the town. Assheton-Smith's agent, Captain N P Stewart, could see the effects on the estate's tenants. At this rate his boss was going to lose income from them. Duff-Ass was persuaded to withdraw his objections. Indeed, it was his daughter, Enid Assheton-Smith, who turned the first sod to begin the laying of the line in 1894.

Recognise the first name?

Yes, it was Enid the sod-turner who gave her name to the redoubtable *Enid*, the puffing pusher that is still going up to the summit and back today.

The British Victorians were never ones to shy away from an engineering challenge and, in 1894, Moon set about employing 150 men who proceeded to blast and chip their way to the top. They built two viaducts and several bridges, sliced out a 100m cutting from solid rock and laid nearly 5 miles of track, exactly 2ft 7½ in wide, up an extraordinarily steep gradient. And they did it in just *14 months.*

Labour was cheap in those days. What was more difficult to acquire was the know-how to run a railway up a mountain. Where would you turn in such circumstances?

The nearest place with specialists in mountain railways was the logical answer. And so it came to pass that the Snowdon Mountain Tramroad and Hotels Co. Ltd came back from Switzerland not only with engines such as *Enid* and *Wydffa*, but also with a special track to run them on. The rack-and-pinion system could just as easily be called the cogwheel-with-teeth railway. Cogwheels under the locomotive engaged with teeth cut into the track to give the train grip and stability. They still do. The system here has worked perfectly well for over 120 years.

Except once.

That 'once' was the opening day. It was 6 April 1896, Easter Monday, and LADAS, otherwise known as Locomotive Number One, was coming down the mountain. Just before Clogwyn, above what is now the Valley of the Hats, the engine was somehow derailed, and plunged over the cliffside. Because it was supporting

Boarding the train at Llanberis soon after the war

rather than pulling, LADAS wasn't coupled to the carriages, and they had an automatic braking system which brought them safely to a halt. Before that happened, however, two passengers had spotted the driver and fireman leap to safety. They decided to try the same. With fatal results in one case. He died from loss of blood.

An inquiry followed, but nothing untoward was found on the track. It was concluded that a spring thaw had eroded the ground beneath, causing LADAS to lurch sideways. On the inquiry's recommendation, the number of passengers was reduced to lower the weight, while grippers and flanged guard rails were installed on either side.

'We haven't had an accident since,' Amanda Ward
assured me as our train now made its way back down
the mountain, before turning away from the lengthy
line of walkers on the right-hand side and gesturing
to the wide open spaces to the left. 'That's where
I walk,' she said dreamily. 'There's a lovely lake on
the other side of that ridge,' she added, before going
on to tell me how her mother and grandmother used
to walk up Snowdon on the night when the harvest
moon was at its fullest, and wait for the dawn. 'I've
done it myself three times, and it's absolutely stunning
watching the sun come up spilling pink and purple on
the peaks.'

No trains at that time. No crowds either. Quite an
experience, I'm sure. All the same, I felt grateful that Sir
Richard Moon had finally triumphed in the long-
running wrangle over the laying of this line, and that so
many men had put in so much backbreaking work to
complete it. The Snowdon Mountain railway remained
a godsend for those of us who have always wanted to
take in one of the finest views imaginable, but have
neither the knees nor the inclination to climb 4.7 miles
up gruelling gradients.

What's more, we never had to carry a stick.

6

THE FIRST RAILWAY ADVENTURE

THE TALYLLYN RAILWAY

Oh, the joys of family life. You see both sides on narrow-gauge lines – the real joys of extended families relaxed in each other's company, and the ironic 'joys' when one little darling or another gives the impression that he or she would rather be somewhere else. Anywhere else.

It was just after 10.30 on a damp and blustery Monday morning. The vivid hanging baskets on Tywyn Wharf Station were swinging in the wind, as though waving us off, while the young teenager in our carriage was having a strop. 'For God's sake, it's too long,' she grumped on being told that we'd be at the end of the line in Nant Gwernol by 11.25 and back here at 12.57. If, that is, the family decided to catch the first train back. There would have been plenty to detain them. Walks through the glorious countryside in the adjoining valley for one thing; the chance to explore the remains of the lead mine for another. Luckily nobody told her that. Otherwise she might have tried to hurl herself on to the rails.

As it was, she was glowering at her phone and prodding it fiercely while her mother stroked her hair in what I assumed was an attempt to calm her down. It seemed to work. The girl shut her eyes – only to open them a minute later when her father pulled on one of those leather window straps.

'*Daa-aaad!*' she almost screamed.

He shrugged. 'If you don't have the windows open, you can't smell the steam.'

Grandad joined in at this point, looking up from perusing the local paper and proudly proclaiming: 'It was all steam in my day. The only disadvantage with steam is when you go through long tunnels. It stinks,' he predicted, just before we plunged into the first of two tunnels at the top of a steepish slope. Mother and daughter raised their eyes to the ceiling.

I did, too, not out of despair or boredom, but because there was rather a lot to admire. The ceiling of our carriage was beamed, like the snug of a country pub. It came as no surprise to read that the Talyllyn line had kept its original carriages, built for the most part by Brown, Marshalls and Co. from Birmingham in the 1860s, using oak frames with mahogany-panelled bodies. Nicely padded leather seats too.

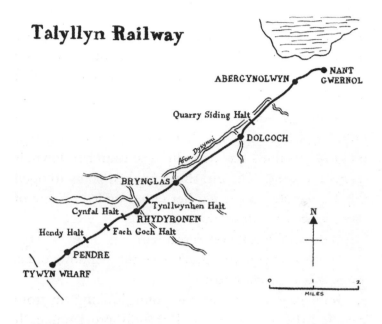

Talyllyn Railway

NANT G-WERNOL

ABERGYNOLWYN

Quarry Siding Halt

DOLGOCH

Afon Dysynni

BRYNGLAS

Tynllwynhen Halt

Cynfal Halt

RHYDYRONEN

Hendy Halt   Fach Goch Halt

N

PENDRE

TYWYN WHARF

0   1   2
MILES

Kneeling on one of them was a wildly excited little girl, about seven or eight years younger than the stroppy teenager. And nearby was a little boy with a peaked cap and a toy monkey. His own excitement was somewhat subdued when a small elderly lady with a large dog joined us at Pendre, the station that also housed the railway's locomotive and carriage sheds. 'He's very well behaved,' she assured the boy, who abandoned his monkey and tentatively stroked the dog, to the evident satisfaction of both. So here was intergenerational conflict in one part of the carriage, and intergenerational bonding in another, as elderly lady and small boy chatted amicably while the dog slipped into a doze, lulled perhaps by the rhythmic *clickety-clack* of the train. To the left of

Talyllyn *on Dolgoch Viaduct* c.1900

us, meanwhile, a tractor was hurtling across a field – hurtling by tractor standards, that is. Was the driver trying to race us? Or was I just imagining it?

For my third (or was it my fourth?) narrow-gauge railway in North Wales I'd doubled back southwards, down the coast beyond Porthmadog and round the Dovey estuary to Tywyn. If the Ffestiniog was the line that in the 19th century really invented the idea of narrow-gauge railways as we know them, the Talyllyn is the one that in the 20th invented the idea of preserving them and keeping them open. The engine pulling us today was even named after the man who, more than any other, had in 1951 been the prime mover in saving this line from closure: Tom Rolt, writer, railway and canal enthusiast. More on him later.

I'd read somewhere that the rescue of the Talyllyn inspired *The Titfield Thunderbolt*, which rolled off the Ealing Comedy production line two years later. There's a famous race in the film in which the train, saved from extinction by the local villagers, takes on a coach run by the dastardly local bus company. And the train wins, albeit narrowly. As the name implies, the *Thunderbolt* could travel at a fair old lick. Considerably faster than the *Tom Rolt*, which took the best part of an hour to cover 7.25 miles. Admittedly, it stopped to pick up more passengers at regular intervals, and was running on a gauge of just 2ft 3in up some steep gradients. Still, as anyone who has driven in rural Wales will confirm, it's always nice to leave a tractor trailing in your wake.

At Rhydyronen Station we were joined by Claire Perkins and Martin Mitchell and their corgi, Tia. They lived in Solihull, where Martin was an engineer at Jaguar Land Rover and Claire worked in recruitment, and they were both among the 4,000 or so members of this, what we must now call the world's first heritage railway to be preserved by volunteers. No, they were not among the hundred or so active ones who kept the line running, but they did love walking around here. 'We've been travelling on this line for the past 10 years,' said Claire. 'Not bad for somebody like me who's not really a big railway fan. Of all the trains I've been forced to go on,' she added with a knowing smile, 'this is my favourite.'

It wasn't difficult to see why, although even just in North and Mid-Wales there was more than enough competition. *Tom Rolt* and the beamed carriages behind had been climbing steadily for some time, and you won't be surprised to hear that the countryside beyond the window was becoming more stunning with every passing hundred yards or so. Not even the weather could sully the beauty. The usual characteristics were there in abundance: green hills, steep valleys, lakes, rivers, waterfalls cascading into gorgeous gorges. Plenty of sheep, needless to say (braised mutton for dinner again tonight, methinks).

Why was that tree bent over at an angle of almost 45 degrees to the ground? No doubt it was the result of centuries of blustery buffetings. And why was I almost getting a crick in the neck trying to see to the top of that hill?

Probably because it was a mountain. Cadair Idris is not as high as Snowdon, but it still rises to not far off 3,000ft. Legend has it that anyone who spends a night on the summit will wake up either mad or a poet. Well, among many poetically inspirational views from the train was the Talyllyn Lake at the foot of old Idris. You might even recognise it from your computer. In 2009 a landscape photograph of the lake became the official desktop 'wallpaper' for a Microsoft software package.

By now the stroppy teenager seemed to have forgiven her dad and quietened down. Indeed, she was almost smiling at the inspirational sights beyond the window. The stations looked attractive, too, with tubs and baskets of flowers and shelters with gleaming paintwork on the gables and drainpipes. Grey, wet slate roofs, of course, and you won't be surprised to learn that slate was the reason for this line's existence in the first place.

Large-scale quarrying began at Bryneglwys, high on the plateau above the station we had just pulled into. ABERGYNOLWYN, it said on one of the benches. Quite a long bench, as it happened, perhaps to accommodate all those letters. The platform was lengthy as well. According to my guidebook, it was one of the longest narrow-gauge platforms in the world. Perhaps they needed the space for all that slate as it waited to be carried down to the wharf at Tywyn for transportation to the wider world.

The Lancashire mill-owner-turned-quarry-magnate William McConnell had the line laid down in the mid-1860s. It was the first purpose-built, steam-worked, narrow-gauge public railway in Britain. An Act of Parliament to allow trains to carry passengers as well as slate was given royal assent in July 1865. Anybody who ventured aboard in the first year and a half did so 'at their own risk' and free of charge. It wasn't until the end of 1866, after minor improvements, that it was given the official stamp of approval. Between 1867 and 1877 the annual passenger traffic doubled to 23,000 a year. The slate trade was booming too. By 1880, Bryneglwys was employing over 300 workers producing over 8,000 tons of finished slabs a year.

I've chronicled the slow demise of the industry from the 1880s already. By 1910 quarry and railway had passed from the McConnell family into the hands of the local landowner, Henry Haydn Jones, who had just become the Liberal MP for Merioneth. He cut costs and safety standards even further in the quarry, but managed to keep it open until 1946. As for the railway, he promised to keep that open until he died and he managed it, just about, thanks to the efforts of his general manager Edward Thomas.

By the time Tom Rolt met him in 1948, Thomas was also 'Secretary, Accountant, Booking Clerk,

Station Master and Guard all rolled into one', wrote Rolt in his book *Railway Adventure*.

'When I first saw him, clad in the neat grey tweed suite he always affects, he was busy selling tickets for the afternoon train at Towyn [now Tywyn] Wharf. When the last passenger had been booked in, he clapped on his trilby hat, locked up the office and walked briskly towards the waiting train with the cash takings in a linen bag tightly clasped by the neck. Before hopping nimbly into the brake van, it was his inevitable custom to signal the 'right way' by a quick, peremptory flick of the wrist of his free hand, as though he were shoo-ing the train away like some disobedient dog...'

Railway Adventure is a detailed account of how the author first came across the line in those grim post-war years, and walked it from Tywyn all the way to Abergynolwyn, taking in the fabulous scenery as well as assessing the sheer volume of repairs and clearance that needed to be done to give a new generation of railway travellers the opportunity to enjoy those views.

Rolt was evidently a persuasive character. When Sir Haydn finally died in July 1950, aged 86, Rolt charmed his widow into donating what was left of the railway to the small army of volunteers that he was beginning to assemble. And in October of the same year, he persuaded a meeting largely made up of Birmingham businessmen to part with some of their hard-earned 'brass' after writing a letter to the *Birmingham Post* and calling a meeting at the city's Imperial Hotel. (At the time the former engineering apprentice-turned-writer was living on a narrow boat on the Worcester and Birmingham Canal.)

The transformation of the line from near-ruin to popular tourist attraction was a resounding success. You can see that all too clearly today. But even when *Railway Adventure* was first published in 1953, Rolt had evidently begun to see the 'invaders' of urban English from the Welsh point of view.

> 'The four coaches would be so packed out by tourists, so resonant with the loud, harsh accents of London, Lancashire, Birmingham or the Black Country, that I would ask the locals to travel with me in the [brake] van. Their soft Welsh voices, quiet good manners, and a friendliness which made me feel one of themselves, were at once a tonic and contrast.'

Brummies, it seemed, were all right for providing cash as long as they kept their traps shut.

Maybe that's a bit hard on Rolt. Like a lot of people who get things done, however, he could sometimes display an abrasive side. 'Certainly he wasn't one to mince his words,' our driver John Scott told me when we reached Nant Gwernol. The line had been extended here from Abergynolwyn in the mid-1970s, by which

Bill Trinder cuts the tape to mark the Preservation Society's takeover of the railway, 1951

Tom Rolt chats to passengers in the Fifties

time John had been coming here from his parents' home in Rutland for 10 years. 'I was 12 when I first travelled on this railway in 1965.'

'And was Rolt still around then?'

'Not very often. He made occasional appearances when I started working here as soon as I was 14. From what I heard, he wasn't always the most diplomatic of people. And I'm told he upset quite a few people in the canal world. Still, fair play to him. If he hadn't called that meeting in Birmingham, we wouldn't be here now.'

John took another bite of his sandwich and a quick swig of tea as we sat on a bench and admired the gleaming green machine that had pulled us here. 'The original engine goes back to the 1940s,' John explained. 'It was one of three built for the Irish Turf Board for the transport of, well, turf. The other two are still in Ireland, but this one eventually found its way here in the late sixties and had to be rebuilt for a different gauge. Although the boiler's original, the frames and plate-work are not. It's the biggest engine here, weighing in at about 14 tons.'

John and two fellow volunteers had started polishing it at 7 o'clock that morning. These days he lived even further away in Cambridge, where he worked as a self-employed design engineer. The drive from the flat Fenlands to the Welsh coast took him about three and three-quarter hours. 'I tend to spend blocks of about four weeks at a time here,' he explained. 'But I also come for the odd weekend every now and then as I'm on one or two committees. Anyway, I haven't missed a year since I started working here in 1967.'

By now it was time for him to climb back in the cab. The 11.40 back to Tywyn Wharf was due to leave soon. This time I decided to brave the hard wooden seats of one of the carriages that were open at the sides. 'I've been colder and wetter,' said a man in an anorak – one of many. In fact, I seemed to be the only person in this carriage without an anorak. Apart, that is, from a teenage boy in a sleeveless shirt and a back-to-front baseball cap. Oh, God, I thought – not another stropper... But no. He turned out to be a rather eloquent young man with a keen interest in politics. 'What you have to remember in these post-Brexit days,' he was telling his parents, 'is that politics isn't between Left and Right any more; it's between open and closed.' His mother looked at him adoringly. His father nodded sagely before resuming the perusal of his somewhat damp copy of the *Telegraph*, seemingly oblivious to the alluring views on either side of the train.

There was a surreal moment when, at one of the loops on the line, an engine with a painted face went past in the opposite direction. Yes, you've guessed it: another character from the seemingly endless works of the Reverend Wilbert Awdry, who seems to have sought much of his inspiration on Welsh narrow-gauge railways. He had been a volunteer here in the 1950s, and based his stories of the Skarloey Railway on the

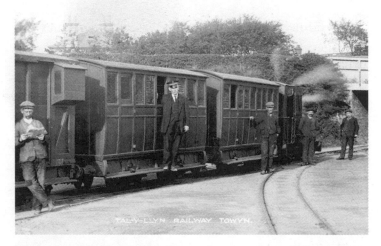

Train at Tywyn Wharf, 1916

Dolgoch takes water at Dolgoch, 1941

Talyllyn line. There were models of Skarloey locos and carriages in the railway's museum down at Tywyn Wharf, as well as a reconstruction of part of his study using the original furniture, donated by his family.

Another writer with a passionate interest in railways was, of course, Sir John Betjeman. To add to the statue at St Pancras, there was a plaque to commemorate him at Tywyn Wharf. Betjeman had been 'the first member of the Talyllyn Railway Preservation Society'. In his foreword to Rolt's book he wrote the following:

'While those levellers, the clerks of British Railways, are shutting down all the beautiful little country branch lines instead of devising a practical means of keeping them open, while they are killing the independent pride of companies, while they are doing away with individual liveries and stamping their same ugly emblem on every engine, while they are concentrating only on express trains and selling the pass to the uncomfortable, unaccommodating, dangerous and hideous bus companies, the Talyllyn Railway is a working witness of the new revolution. Had the Talyllyn been included in 'British Railways', this experiment could never have been made. We "own" British Railways but we are allowed no say in them. We really do own the Talyllyn Railway. Perhaps its example will put life into the dead hand of British Railways and help to save our remaining branch lines.'

Some hope!

That foreword was written in June 1953, nearly a decade before the BR chairman known universally as 'Doctor' Beeching began his radical surgery on many a survivor. Since then, of course, we have had the privatisation of the railways, which has hardly led to a return of Betjeman's 'beautiful little country branch lines'. Why should the private companies even consider it if they're not profitable?

All the more reason, then, to celebrate the survival and revival of narrow-gauge railways such as the Talyllyn. Putting up with the occasional teenage strop is neither here nor there.

7

THE LAST
NARROW-GAUGE
ON BRITISH RAIL

THE VALE OF RHEIDOL RAILWAY

The satnav wouldn't always talk to me in North Wales. Perhaps she was sulking. 'What do you expect with all these mountains?' she may have been muttering under her breath for all I knew. The Vale of Rheidol Railway's station in Aberystwyth was supposed to be close to the mainline station, but stumbling across it had more to do with luck than computer-driven judgement from the heavens. I found it at the far end of an enormous car park behind a branch of Matalan. At one time there had been a cattle market and slaughterhouse on the site. Those were the days when British shops still sold largely British-made goods and retail parks such as the one beyond Matalan were something of a rarity. Timber and ore transported by the narrow-gauge line from the Rheidol Valley were

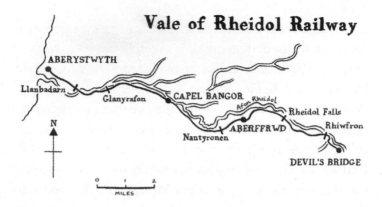

either transferred to the wider network or sent on by branch line to the port beyond.

British manufacturing was already on the slide by the mid-1960s, although there were still plenty of coal mines, and Wales had more than its fair share – hence the need for timber from the pine forests up in the nearby hills for all those pit-props. This Vale of Rheidol line, not quite 2ft wide and not quite 12 miles long, had finally opened in 1902. I say 'finally' because lack of finance had delayed the laying of the track for four years. To save money, rock had to be hewn by pick-axe instead of being blasted.

If freight from the lead mine up the line at Rhiwfron eventually declined, at least there was a growing demand from holidaymakers to travel through the magnificent landscape between Aberystwyth and Devil's Bridge. The first passengers were on board within four months of the line opening for business. Tourism and timber became the Rheidol railway's key to survival, but its ultimate success was down to tourism alone. The Great Western realised that quickly enough when it took it over in 1922, and unlike many a narrow-gauge line, the Vale of Rheidol closed only briefly during World War II. Even British Rail allowed steam trains to continue here after decreeing that they should run out of steam everywhere else on the network by 1968. Barbara Castle accepted an invitation to make a trip on the line during her period as Minister of Transport in the 1960s, and it's easy to see why she was persuaded to allow British Rail to keep it chugging along.

The Vale of Rheidol was, however, the first part of the network to be privatised, as long ago as 1989. It was bought by Peter Rampton and Tony Hills, now the owner and general manager of the Brecon Mountain Railway – yet, another, but much more recent, narrow-gauge railway in Wales. Rampton and Hills having split their partnership in 1996, by which time the privatisation of the rest of the network was nearing completion, the Vale of Rheidol is now run by a trust. It is still run entirely by professionals.

Reverting to private ownership also allowed the reversion to Great Western colours for the rolling stock and the passenger facilities on the immaculately maintained stations across the valley – an irresistible combination, judging by the numbers who were travelling today. OK, it was tourist season in early August but, having persuaded my wife to join me on this journey, I found there hardly seemed to be a spare

Passengers embark at Devil's Bridge during British Railways days

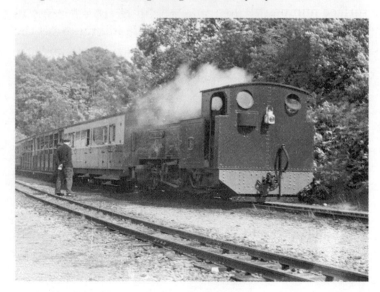

A Vale of Rheidol Railway train pauses at Aberffrwd loop

seat available. Eventually we managed to squeeze onto the 1.30 out of Aberystwyth, and found ourselves almost knee-to-knee with the couple opposite.

Ben and Susan Williams, it transpired, lived just over the Welsh side of the Shropshire border in a house over a tunnel on the main line. 'We love railways,' said Susan. Just as well, perhaps. Ben, a founder member of the Llangollen Railway Society, had just pulled on one of those seasoned leather straps to open the window and sniff the steam. 'Oh, the smell of Welsh smoke,' he almost purred. Yes, deep mining has ceased in Wales as it has elsewhere in the UK. This small island, standing on sizeable seams of coal, chooses to import the stuff from various distant parts of the globe. But some surface mining still goes on, particularly in the south of the Principality, and Ben could evidently tell from the smell the difference between its black gems and the common-or-garden stuff brought in from Siberia or Colombia or wherever. He could also tell me the last time he had travelled on this line. 'It was 1964 when I was 11. British Rail in those days, of course, and the engines were a horrible shade of blue. None of these buildings were here then,' he added, gesturing beyond the window to some light industrial units on the outskirts of Aberystwyth.

Suddenly a cricket pitch came into view. 'Ooh, look!' said Susan. 'One of the fielding team's waving to us.' Mmm. Not sure about that. It looked to me as though the captain was gesturing to the fielder at mid-wicket to move a little deeper.

The line was straight at this point. Surprisingly so for a narrow-gauge railway. In fact, the Capel Bangor Straight, as it's known, went on for about a mile and a quarter, passing through some woodland in full summer leaf. To mis-quote Shakespeare, 'Summer's leaf hath all too short a date', but I'm sure those abundant trees would look even more attractive in autumnal browns and golds.

My musing was interrupted by a child at the back of the carriage who had been spooked by a wasp, and was reacting with wildly flapping arms and legs. Not to mention loud shrieks, much to the evident embarrassment of his parents. Heaven knows how he would have reacted had he been stung. Wasps in August: whatever next? Luckily, the striped intruder buzzed off out of a window and calm was restored as we pulled into Capel Bangor Station. The colour of the corrugated iron shelters here received nods of approval from Ben and Susan. Just the right shades for a Great Western line, apparently. My wife was more impressed by the Victorian lamp-posts and the glowing flower beds that lit up this and other stations along the line. So was I, if truth be told, although I liked to pretend that I knew something about the Great Western. The gardeners, I'd been told, were all volunteers. One of them was waving to us now, taking a break from a little light weeding.

No sooner had we left the station, it seemed, than we passed through a large dairy farm. For listeners to *The Archers* it was as though we had briefly had a glimpse of Brookfield. No sign of David or Ruth, Pip or Josh, but the cows made a change from sheep, and there were even a couple of horses galloping away from us in some alarm. Ben broke off from a short lecture on double-funnelled engines to point out that we were just coming up to a 1 in 48 incline.

Indeed, from now on the line climbed at an incredible rate. We stopped briefly for water at Nantyronen. Or should that be 'Nantyronnen'? 'There should be another "n" before the last one,' Ben insisted, after both he and Susan had noted disapprovingly that the shelters here were not quite the right shade.

By the time we reached Aberffrwd Station we were 280ft above sea level. The train had climbed 266ft in 7 miles since leaving Aberystwyth, and the retail park beyond Matalan seemed to belong to a different planet. For the last four miles of the journey, we were apparently going up at a rate of a hundred feet every mile. And the view seemed to become more spectacular with every passing minute.

The Vale of Rheidol is, by all accounts, a great place to look out for birds of prey. Susan not only knew about railways, she could also tell me the difference between a kite and a buzzard. Being about as good a twitcher as I am a trainspotter, I saw neither. What I could see were wispy pink flowers clinging to the rocks, the sun shimmering on the surface of rivers and lakes, and what looked like a few toy houses miles below us as we passed over a hillside ridge known as Pant Mawr, just wide enough to accommodate the width of this narrow-gauge train. The train itself – or rather the engine – could be seen through the trees as it followed the contours of the land around what is known as 'the Horseshoe' in English and Cwmyr Ogos in its native tongue.

Here and there were signs of man-made intrusions across this stirring landscape. On one side was a hydro-electric dam and reservoir, as well as the Rheidol Power Station which supplied green energy to Aberystwyth and the surrounding area. On the other side were legacies of the mining industry. There was a spoil tip known locally as 'the Stag' because that's the shape it seems to represent, and, further up the line, as the train climbed higher and higher, were the remains of the Cwmrheidol lead mine. It was closed in the 1930s and only the toxic waste heaps remain.

We parted company with Ben and Susan at Pontarfynach, otherwise known as Devil's Bridge. I'm sure they would have gone to check out the ticket office, built in 1901 and the only original building left on the line. For us it was time to go looking for that fabled bridge. Before leaving the flatlands of Aberystwyth, I'd been told about the connection with the devil by the splendidly named Sophia de Rochefort, who sounded like a character from Jane Austen or

Downton Abbey but turned out to be a former student, originally from Cornwall, who had never seen a steam train before dropping out of Aberystwyth University and joining the Vale of Rheidol's marketing department. This is what she'd said:

'There are three bridges, seemingly built one on top of the other. The bottom one was said to have been built by the devil himself. A woman whose cow was stuck on the other side of the river was said to have made a deal with him. He planned to take the soul of the first living being who stepped across the bridge, expecting it to be the woman herself. But she saw through him and threw some bread across the bridge which her dog promptly followed.'

Maybe that dog is still burning in the fires of hell. The cow as well, perhaps, resulting in a somewhat overdone steak to go with a hot dog. The more likely explanation is that the bridge was built by monks from the nearby Strata Florida Abbey in the 11th century. Built to last, when you came to think about it, as that bridge must be approaching its thousandth birthday. We could just about see it beyond the two bridges built since as we gazed down from the road into the Mynach Falls, where the gurgle of spilling water echoed from far below. Somewhere down there the River Mynach dropped some 295ft into the River Rheidol. Another spectacular view. A chance to take a closer look, what's more, if you paid a small charge to go down innumerable steps.

We decided against it. After all, we had a train to catch and we both fancied a cup of tea. So we strolled back past the drinkers enjoying the mid-afternoon sunshine outside the Three Bridges Hotel. On the way we passed a shop selling exotic-looking chocolates. My wife looked as though the devil himself had dropped temptation in her way. But she managed to resist it, and we sat on one of many benches outside the station cafe sipping our cuppas and, in my case, pondering an old line from Jerome K. Jerome: 'I like work; it fascinates me. I could sit and watch it all day.'

Jerome was the author of *Three Men in a Boat*, while I was watching two men and a train. Driver Chris Harris and fireman Jack Smith were polishing that green and black GWR engine, *Llewellyn*, within an inch of its life. Even the coal gleamed. The engine was built by Davies and Metcalfe, founded at the Rheidol Foundry in Aberystwyth in 1878 but long since decamped to Stockport. And the coal? Well, as Ben had already sniffed out, that too had its origins somewhere in Wales.

Chris turned out have an unlikely background for a train driver. His early years had been spent in Lancashire and he had wanted to be a vet when he grew up. But somehow he finished up at Huddersfield University where he studied music technology. 'Mind you, I've always been interested in anything that moved,' he told me during a brief break from polishing. 'My uncle got me interested in the Ffestiniog Railway, and I worked

Capel Bangor station during Great Western Railway days before the war

A train enters a passing loop in British Railways days

there during the holidays from the age of 13. I became a trainee driver on my 21st birthday, first as a volunteer at Ffestiniog. Then I moved here to take a full-time job. You have to work as a fireman for four years, watching what the drivers do.'

'Hot work,' I suggested.

'Well, it's 200 degrees in that firebox but, of course, the boiler is lagged. Still, all you can do on a hot day like this is to stick your head out of the cabin every now and then,' he added before returning to cleaning duties. Sophia had already given me a glimpse of the engine shed to which this gleaming, steaming machine would eventually return. The place had been immaculate. I'd never seen a shed so neat and tidy. Even the spanners were arranged on the wall in descending order of size. Piles of wood were stacked in beautifully polished wheelbarrows. And those 1920s GWR carriages that weren't on duty looked as though they might have been painted the day before – in a shade, I'm sure, that would have passed muster with Ben and Susan.

We didn't travel with them on the way back. Instead we decided go al fresco, or at least find a seat in one of the carriages with open sides. Easier said than done. Not because of weight of numbers but because of the weight and width of some of the passengers.

The more I travelled around this small island by little train, the more conscious I became that it has more than its fair share of large people. Consider the blonde woman taking up so much of one bench that there was just about room for her small son to snuggle up next to her. I managed to squeeze on to the bench behind, and my wife on to the one behind that.

It turned out they were part of a large family of at least four generations. From Birmingham, by the sound of it, and they were having a high old time. Grandad, sporting a Bob Dylan T-shirt, was holding court every now and then. But the laughter wasn't for him alone, and there was an easiness between the generations that struck me as quite touching. Travelling by narrow-gauge railway had already given me a heartening sense that the extended family is far from dead, and here was further evidence.

The open-carriage journey was far more in-your-face. Literally so. A brisk breeze brought the fresh air of this delightful valley into hair, cheeks and nostrils. And from here we had an even better view of *Llewellyn* as the locomotive wove its way between trees and bracken-bedecked banks. There was a somewhat unnerving moment when the entire party of Brummies, including the sizeable ones, surged to one side of the carriage to gaze down from the steep Pant Mawr ridge and take photos with their phones.

Thankfully, we stayed on track, and enjoyed the views as well as the raucous conversation, while down, down we went towards the much flatter outskirts of Aberystwyth. The family's Jack Russell pricked up its ears and growled menacingly as we chugged through the dairy farm. Perhaps it could smell a rat. One word from Grandad, however, and it quietened down. We passed a circus tent, from which was emanating the incongruous rhythm of the can-can. To the left, the cricket match was still going on, and now another captain was waving frantically.

8

THE RAILWAY THAT CAME BACK FROM THE DEAD

THE WELSH HIGHLAND RAILWAY

Five Welsh trains in five days, and this was to be the last. And the longest by far. All the narrow-gauge railways hereabouts liked to have some claim to fame, and the Welsh Highland couldn't pitch itself as the oldest or the highest or the world's first. Well, the Welsh Highland wasn't just the longest in Wales; it was and still is 'the longest heritage railway in the UK'. So there. What's more, it ran 'the most powerful narrow-gauge steam engines in the world'.

Well, that figured, I suppose. If you were going to travel 25 miles hauling at least 10 carriages on 'some of the longest and steepest gradients in the UK', then you were going to need a big 'un, so to speak. Just to cap it all, it not only passed Snowdon (been there, done that), it travelled through the Aberglaslyn Pass, voted 'the

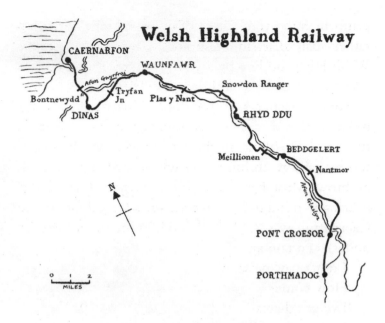

most beautiful spot in the UK' by members of the National Trust.

Heaven knows how the Trust members worked that one out. I can well believe that the most beautiful part of the UK is in North Wales, but there's a fair amount of competition in these parts, as I'd been privileged to witness over the past five days. Anyway, I looked forward to seeing the Pass and, indeed, Caernarfon Castle at the end of the line.

Pity about the weather. It was grey and drizzly. Very different from the glorious sunshine in which I'd basked last time I was here on Porthmadog Station on – when was it? – oh, yes, Friday afternoon. Same station, different platform, mind you. Those of us bound for Caernarfon rather than Blaenau Ffestiniog were escorted to the Welsh Highland line by a young volunteer dressed in a black frock coat, like an Edwardian butler.

Some passengers on the 9.40 didn't need showing, because they'd done this journey before. Thirteen times in 2016 alone, in the case of Malcolm Brooks, a serious railway enthusiast, heavy of jowl and bushy of eyebrow. 'Must have cost you a fortune,' I suggested, bearing in mind that the return adult fare all the way to Caernarfon was £38. Well, £34.20 for those over (or under) a certain age.

'I don't pay,' he said.

'How come?'

'I've got shares.'

'In the railway?'

'That's right.'

Conversations with Malcolm tended to be short and to the point, I discovered on the two-hour-25-minute journey. That was partly because he gave the impression of being a no-nonsense northerner (north of England, that is), and partly because he was busy looking out of the window, opening it at critical moments to see beyond the streaks of drizzle. A few smoky clouds emitted from the funnel didn't bother him. Like a lot of buffs, he evidently revelled in the stuff. A railway reference book was bulging out of his pocket. He also had an umbrella and a knapsack and seemed to know exactly those moments when the line would bend and

Constructing Cutting Mawr on the Welsh Highland above Beddgelert, 1920s

the engine would come into view – a great, gleaming brute of a thing seemingly ploughing through the bracken as it wound its way, this way and that, across the Snowdonia National Park.

This time our route out of Harbour Station would not be eastwards across the Cob towards the Boston lodge works, but straight out along the road. Well, not straight for long. The Welsh Highland was a very rare line in that – just as it had been when it was first built – the first short section through the town ran on tracks embedded into the tarmac of the High Street (the traffic being stopped either side in the manner of a level crossing). The rails still went through an S-bend across the road; then the train curved to the right off onto its own dedicated route across the plain and northwards up into the hills towards Snowdonia. When it wasn't smothered in cloud, as it was that day, you could apparently see the peak of Snowdon first on your right, then on your left, then on your right again.

'I've walked this line, you know,' Malcolm suddenly confided.

'All the way?'

'Almost. We did it in stages, three or four miles at a time.'

'We?'

'Myself and a friend who's sadly no longer with us.'

'Why did you walk it?'

'We wanted to follow the line as they were rebuilding it.'

That would have been in the nineties and the noughties, the Ffestiniog Railway having bid for the trackbed in 1989 and acquired the assets from the Official Receiver in 1995. Plus a Lottery grant of £4.3 million. To relate how it all came about, I'd better refer back to the conversation I'd had with Andrew Thomas of the Ffestiniog and Welsh Highland Railways when I'd been at Porthmadog Station five days previously. Over to you, Andrew:

'The Welsh Highland was originally built on the success of the Ffestiniog, but considerably later. It didn't open until 1923, well past the peak of the slate industry. The line quickly became known as a white elephant. It made very little profit, and had lots of loans from local authorities along the way. So what money it did make went towards paying the interest on those loans. It went bust after 13 years. The Ffestiniog tried to revive it, and kept it going for another three years, but it was still losing money, as the 1930s depression was hitting the tourist industry as well as the slate trade.'

The war was the final straw or, more accurately, the final slate. No more exports to Germany. End of slate trade. End of two narrow-gauge lines. For the time being, at least.

As anyone who has read one of the previous chapters will know, the Ffestiniog was rebuilt and re-laid by volunteers in the 1950s and eventually became a resounding commercial success. Unlike the Ffestiniog,

A pre-war line-up of station staff at Harbour Station in Porthmadog

An early postcard of Porthmadog, showing the Cob to the right

however, after closure the Welsh Highland Railway had all its track torn up; there was very little of it left on the trackbed snaking its way across the landscape. Here's Andrew again:

'Rumours began to emerge that somebody wanted to rebuild it. What the Ffestiniog didn't want was competition from a longer line. The attitude was: "We'd better do it ourselves."'

Easier said than done.

'The main problem was trying to consolidate the trackbed. It had been abandoned but never officially closed, because the official receiver had died on the day he was due to sign it off. The last directors had also died in the meantime. In the end, a firm called Trackbed Consolidation Ltd had to go round, find all the surviving shareholders from the original company, and consolidate the shareholding until they had a majority. Then we could put in for an Act of Parliament and rebuild the whole railway.'

Work began in earnest in 1997, and was completed by 2011. With a vital three-mile extension to Caernarfon, what's more. 'One of the reasons why the Welsh Highland had been useless for tourism was that it didn't go to where people wanted to go,' Andrew had told me – originally its northern terminus had been where it met the main line running west out of Caernarfon, at an obscure station called Dinas Junction. That British Rail line having itself long since closed, the new Welsh Highland could extend along its old trackbed all the way into the tourist hub of Caernarfon, to terminate right underneath the historic castle. 'The line now makes slightly more profit per mile than even the Ffestiniog, because the journey's long enough to be able to offer cooked meals.'

Back on the 9.40 I was having the occasional surreptitious glance at the menu while inhaling appetising blasts of smoke every time Malcolm opened the window and instructed me to 'Look at that'. Yes, despite the persistent drizzle, the scenery was as fabulous as ever. What's more, the mountains, gorges, forests, lakes, waterfalls and moss-encrusted rocky banks went on for miles and miles. A bit more detail later, I promise. First I just wanted to contemplate what I might fancy to eat on the return journey. Not a 'Welsh Beef Madras', that's for sure, even when 'served on a bed of wild rice with a crispy poppadom and mango chutney'. Too hot for my liking, a Madras, Welsh or otherwise. On reflection, the 'Welsh' bit of that dish evidently referred to the origins of the beef. Made a change from mutton or lamb, I suppose.

I'd seen off a full English – sorry, a full Welsh breakfast (minus a sausage or two) at our B&B that morning, so I wasn't remotely interested in one of the bacon sandwiches that another frock-coated young volunteer was conveying down the carriage from the kitchen area next door. But I was conscious that we had a long car journey ahead once we finally returned to the car park at Porthmadog station later in the

A rather ramshackle train stops for water in the early days of the Welsh Highland Railway

The railway bridge at Bryn-y-Felin

The Leighton Buzzard Light Railway

Triumph *on the elevated section of the Sittingbourne and Kemsley Light Railway*

Speeding across Romney Marsh on the Romney, Hythe and Dymchurch Railway

One of the Ffestiniog Railway's Double Fairlies on the way down to Porthmadog

Re-creating a gravity slate train on the Ffestiniog Railway

Clockwise from left: Eighty-year-old Mike Todd dispatches a train at Harbour Station; Winter on the Cob; Up in the hills towards Blaenau Ffestiniog

Pushing the train on its long slow journey up Snowdon

The precipitous gradient on the Snowdon Mountain Railway

Dolgoch Viaduct on the Talyllyn Railway

Edward Thomas *framed by Welsh daffodils at Rhydyronen on the Talyllyn Railway*

A distant view of Cader Idris beyond the Talyllyn Railway

A train hugs the forested hillside as it climbs towards Devil's Bridge on the Vale of Rheidol Railway

A Vale of Rheidol Railway train at Alt Ddu

The little steam train is tiny against the stunning sweep of the Vale of Rheidol

One of the Welsh Highland Railway's huge Garratt locos crosses the Afon Glaslyn at Pont Croesor

Bluebells near Beddgelert on the Welsh Highland Railway

Pakis Baru No.1, *a former sugar plantation locomotive, prepares to take a bulk seed train around the* demonstration line at the Statfold Barn Railway

Graham Lee's remarkable collection of narrow-gauge locomotives in the Roundhouse at Statfold Barn

Jerry M *through the shed doorway at the Statfold Barn Railway*

Farm
track
near
Grindon
high
above
Manifold
valley

The Manifold Way, formerly the trackbed of the Leek and Manifold Valley Light Railway

Not the Manifold Way!!
That's in a deep valley!

On the turntable at the Ravenglass and Eskdale Railway

The Lakeland fells provide a backdrop as two trains cross on the Ravenglass and Eskdale Railway

Three locomotives at the railway works at Ravenglass

Barber *hauls a South Tynedale Railway train across the Gilderdale Viaduct*

Three views of the Bure Valley Railway in the Norfolk Broads

A footbridge nowadays marks where the Southwold Railway used to cross the river at Blythburgh

Lyd, an exact replica of one of the original Lynton and Barnstaple Railway locomotives, hauls restored carriages on the reopened line to Woody Bay

The Ffestiniog Railway's Blanche *visits the Lynton and Barnstaple Railway in 2015*

The little Leadhills and Wanlockhead Railway train stands at Leadhills Station

The mining past of the line is plain to see in this view of a freight train

afternoon. So what about the Welsh Rarebit on the return journey? 'Welsh' in this case is a term used all over the UK. But this particular rarebit promised 'strong cheese, mustard and ale with our chef's grandmother's secret addition'.

Somebody eventually came in to inform us that there wouldn't be any hot food on the way back because 'the chef's decided to stay on in Caernarfon'. Perhaps he needed to consult with his grandmother. Ah, well. Sandwiches on the way back then.

'It's brightening up a bit,' somebody at the front of the carriage announced. She turned out to be one of those lovely ladies who always look on the bright side. I assumed (wrongly, as it turned out) that she might have been a teacher at one time. It was something to do with the way she enthused and informed those around her – in this case her nine-year-old granddaughter and two friends. 'That's the look-out point for ospreys,' she was telling them. 'They nest in that wood. I saw it on *Countryfile*.'

We had stopped at the first station out of Porthmadog, Pont Croesor, where the RSPB had a watch point. From there you could look through a telescope at these rare ospreys' nest. 'I can see the hides but no ospreys,' I told her by way of introduction. 'Mind you, perhaps it's unlikely on a day like this.'

'Yes, we're only going as far as Beddgelert, having a spot of lunch and catching the 2.30 back,' she told me, before asking me if I knew about the last resting place of Gelert, the most famous dog in these parts. She then persuaded one of the children to tell me about it, only intervening when the story went slightly awry. It was a somewhat long and rambling version of events that boiled down to this:

'In the 13th century Llewelyn, prince of North Wales, had a palace at Beddgelert. One day he went hunting without Gelert, "the faithful hound", who was unaccountably absent. On Llewelyn's return the truant, stained and smeared with blood, joyfully sprang to meet his master. The prince, alarmed, hastened to find his son and saw the infant's cot empty, the bedclothes and floor covered with blood. The frantic father plunged the sword into the hound's side, thinking it had killed his heir. The dog's dying yell was answered by a child's cry. Llewelyn searched and discovered the boy unharmed, but nearby lay the body of a mighty wolf which Gelert had slain. The prince, filled with remorse, is said never to have smiled again.'

That's what it says on a stone monument just south of the village. Not that I could read it from the train, of course. I looked it up on the internet later. 'You can just about see the monument from here,' the grandmother-who-was-never-a-teacher told me shortly before disembarking. Well, it's amazing what you learn on narrow-gauge railways. 'Man bites dog: that's news,' as we used to say in newspapers. 'Dog kills wolf: that's the stuff of legends,' we might have added.

Apart from the *Telegraph* reader I'd spotted on the Talyllyn line, very few people read newspapers on narrow-gauge railways. Or looked at laptops or tablets, let alone books. Why would you, when there's so much beauty beyond the window?

'This is like therapy. I feel so at peace when I'm on these narrow-gauge lines,' said a man sporting a Mercedes cap and a T-shirt on which was inscribed the somewhat dubious claim that OLD GUYS RULE. David Carwen turned out to be a spring chicken of 51, a self-employed engineer who lived with his wife Jill in Stoke-on-Trent. 'We did Ffestiniog on a day when it was 38 degrees and the hottest place in the country,' he recalled. 'Since then this one's always been on my tick list. My dad worked on the main line in the Potteries and passed on his love of railways. What I love about them here is that the scenery is so different.'

Very different from Arnold Bennett country, I agreed, as we gazed out at more gorges, lakes, waterfalls and mountains thrusting through low cloud. Perhaps because we would be heading back to reality later in the day, I started to look out for more mundane signs of everyday life – a wet grey-slate roof on a white cottage, some pigs worthy of Tom Archer peering over a corrugated-iron sty, a former stationmaster's house that was now a local CAMRA Pub of the Year, and a campsite full of tents and caravans. As for those great swathes of rosebay willowherb, I've got more than enough of them in my garden, thank you. Mind you, I've got nothing like those banks of bright orange lucifers that seemed to light up the day as the drizzle faded away.

And the National Trust's beloved Aberglaslyn Pass? As you might expect, that turned out to be anything but mundane. We passed over a ledge cut into the foothills of yet another great swathe of steepness. Below us the River Glaslyn wound its way foamingly over jutting boulders. On the far bank, the tree-covered lower slopes seemed even greener than usual in high summer – a contrast, perhaps, with the grey rocks above as they clambered away towards yet another gateway to the clouds.

My reverie was interrupted by the woman behind cooing: 'You've got a clean botty now.'

Yes, of course, she was talking to her baby. Her father, meanwhile, was sitting across the gangway, slightly apart from the rest of the family where he could revel in the views. David Stubbs, a retired carpenter and joiner from Gillingham, also worked on the Kent and East Sussex Railway, where he had been a guard for the past 40 years. 'Now I'm restoring an engine from scrapyard condition.'

'So why come all the way up here to travel on another railway?'

'Because there's so much to see here. Ours is nothing like this. It's very… well, very southeast England. Mind you, both lines had one thing in common: they were both managed by Colonel Stephens at one time.' Like many another up and down this small island.

The unlikely son of an art critic and Pre-Raphaelite Brotherhood member, Col. Holman Stephens managed the Welsh Highland in its earliest days. But not even he could make it pay. He died aged 62 in 1931, four years before the railway shut for the first time. By then he was back in Kent, at the Lord Warden Hotel in Dover. He was also alone, having no wife and no heir. His estate of £30,000, a small fortune at the time, was bequeathed to four of the staff at Tonbridge Station. Not surprisingly, there was some discontent among a lot more of his employees at railways up and down the land.

Back on the Porthmadog to Caernarfon line, Malcolm too seemed slightly discontented. We had just pulled into a station with the unusually English-sounding name of Snowdon Ranger. Originally just called Snowdon, this was the station whose opening had been the catalyst for the building of the Snowdon Mountain Railway to protect Llanberis's tourist trade. Malcolm was peering at his watch with furiously furrowed eyebrows. 'We're running slightly late,' he growled at a passing frock coat. 'Is there a problem with the coal?'

The lad didn't have a clue. At least Malcolm could relax a bit further up the line when we came to a halt.

'Ah,' he said. 'There's the coal.' Welsh open-cast by the look of it, he assured me. None of that foreign muck.

A considerable amount was being transferred by mechanical digger from a great heap of the stuff by the side of the line. No wonder our driver, Keith Frazer, a retired teacher of technology from somewhere near Stockport, looked a little smutty of face when we finally pulled into Caernarfon. 'You need a lot of coal for a big engine like this on a line this long,' he confirmed. The engine seemed to breathe a steamy sigh of concurrence.

It was a truly giant locomotive for a narrow-gauge railway, and if the Double Fairlie looked like two engines joined back to back, this one looked more like a whole train in itself. It was known simply as 143, and had been the last locomotive built in Manchester by Beyer, Peacock and Co, originally for a freight line in South Africa serving the sugar plantations. Two more of these former South African Railways Garratt locos have emerged from the engine sheds at Boston Lodge for use on the Welsh Highland. They, too, are numbered rather than named. They weighed in at over 66 tons, which seems enormous for a gauge of just 2ft or, to be strictly accurate, 1ft 11½in.

Caernarfon's waterfront looked out over the Menai Straits and Anglesey, and the town itself was threaded by fascinating streets. Wales is full of castles, but Caernarfon's was perhaps the most impressive I'd ever clapped eyes on. Appropriately enough, Prince Charles was invested as Prince of Wales within those mighty walls in 1969. But relations between Wales and England were somewhat more strained back in 1282 when Edward I invaded. The following year he ordered the building of the current castle, along with the walled town that it has dominated ever since. Our time there was all too short.

On the return trip to Porthmadog I tried to spot one or two of the many landmarks on this lengthy line I had missed on the way out. The sun was out by now, making the scenery even more dazzling. The handsomely restored station at Tryfan Junction, winner of a National Railway Heritage Award, turned out to be the gateway to the 'Slate Trail'. From there you could follow the former Bryngwyn branch line that once connected the Welsh Highland with the slate quarries on the slopes of Moel Tryfan. Some of those quarries dated back to Roman times, and there were more beyond them. Quite a bit further down the line lay Cnicht, otherwise known as the 'Matterhorn of Wales'. In fact, it's not *that* high by the standards of the Snowdonia National Park, but it's a long ridge that comes to a sharpish peak, and it looked particularly impressive now that the clouds had lifted.

Impressive in a very different way was the Britannia Bridge, gateway to Porthmadog for some two hundred years, although it has been rebuilt in 1922 and strengthened a couple of times since. One minute we were looking down from it at the boats in the harbour, the next we were winding our way across the S-shaped level crossing bordered by crowds of pedestrians. Meanwhile, a young man in a Mr Happy T-shirt with a ponytail and a multi-coloured shoulder bag sat across the gangway from his friends continued to address them at full volume as he had done for the best part of two hours. What Malcolm would have made of it I shudder to think.

9

SHANGRI-LA

THE STATFOLD BARN RAILWAY

Tamworth has its own castle, street market and the country's first full-sized indoor ski slope. With snow. Reliant Robins, immortalised by Del Boy in *Only Fools and Horses*, were made there until 2003. But to me the town will always hold memories of steam trains. The station is on the junction of two lines running roughly north–south and east–west, and trainspotters flocked to its station in the school holidays back in the late 1950s and early sixties. And maybe for some years after that, for all I know.

I gave up trainspotting when I was 10 or 11. OK, 12 at the most. Coming from the south side of Birmingham, I would catch a train into town with a few mates, change platforms at New Street and head for that Staffordshire Shangri-La where I think I once caught sight of *Britannia* flying through. Or was it the *Royal Scot*? What I *can* remember, and have always been grateful for, is that kids of my generation had the freedom to roam.

I was briefly back home in the Midlands after spending an unforgettable week in North Wales. I'd ridden on a quaint little line frozen in time known as the Talyllyn, a huge narrow-gauge line called the Welsh Highland, a train that just went straight up a mountain, the railway across the Vale of Rheidol whose steam trains had just kept on chugging up and down no matter who owned it, whether industries closed or war broke out. Not fforgetting the Ffestiniog, which managed to combine gravity slate trains from the 19th century, civil engineering projects to put Network Rail to shame, a white-bearded octogenarian volunteer who looked like a stationmaster, and a global travel agency. All in one little corner of this island, and all amidst the most magnificent, sylvan, mountainous landscapes. What's more, my wife had been with me for the whole trip. Not that she shares my new-found interest in out-of-the-way railways any more than my love of cricket, football history, rugby and real ale. But she did travel on two of the lines, savouring the scenery and, as a former social worker, revelling in the sight of so many happy families enjoying each other's company as well as the journeys.

Now, for the next leg of my travels, I wasn't going far afield at all – not much more than 25 miles, in fact, and back to an old stamping-ground.

Birmingham New Street is now a glitzy shopping centre with railway lines underneath it. But at least you

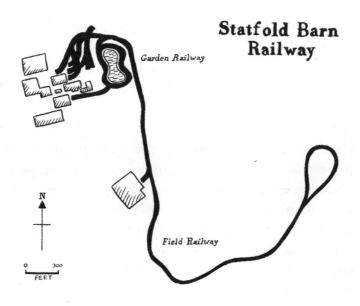

Statfold Barn Railway

Garden Railway

N

0   300
FEET

Field Railway

can get a decent cup of coffee before setting off on the
sometimes baffling search for the right platform. Trains
travelling southwest will pass through suburban Brum
at its best, with expansive parkland and the back gardens
of expensive houses rolling down to the green banks of
an attractive canal. On a grim, grey and drizzly Saturday
morning, however, the line running northeast towards
Tamworth was not designed to evoke happy memories.
Goods yards gave way to scrapyards, the ruins of former
engineering works, the stained concrete of high-rise
flats and motorway flyovers. Huge pylons dwarfed
whatever scrubby-looking trees there were until
suddenly we were out into open countryside. It was
the flattish country that's prevalent in this part of

Midland England, but green and pleasant all the same. Cows were lying down in fields bordered by narrow lanes and, in one case, a canal. Not that this comparative idyll lasted long. Soon we were passing through estates of relatively modern housing that heralded the borders of Tamworth.

Today I was headed for a new railway Shangri-la, and the sheer scale of the narrow-gauge extravaganza that awaited began to dawn on me when I joined the taxi queue outside the station. Nick Britton, a former water engineer, had come all the way from Farnham in Surrey. 'Had to get up at six this morning,' he confided, 'but I wouldn't miss one of these open days for the world.'

'Pity about the weather,' I remarked, the drizzle by now having settled into a steady downpour. It was chilly, too. Autumn seemed to have arrived early.

'This is nothing.' Nick shrugged. 'It snowed on the day they opened in March three years ago, but I made it all the way up and all the way back without a minute's lateness.'

'And the open day? Did it stay "open"?'

'Some of the drivers couldn't get in because of the weather, but it carried on with only eight engines.'

Note that 'only'. Like Nick, I had shelled out a tenner for an invitation to this, the third and final open day of the year. The directions were printed on the back. I was about to show them to the taxi driver, but it quickly became apparent that she didn't need showing. Evidently she had done this journey umpteen times already that morning.

Perhaps a little history (and geography) is required at this point. Statfold Barn is three miles or so out of town, set in God knows how many acres of former farmland, and surrounded by flattish Staffordshire countryside even more attractive than the all-too-brief oasis of greenery between Birmingham and Tamworth. There were rather more people here, however. Considerably more, in fact. They were filing down the long, straight drive, milling around the stalls beyond the car park, queuing patiently at temporary stations and chatting amicably and, in some cases excitedly, like old friends at an annual reunion.

Statfold Barn is the home of Graham Lee, his wife Carol, their private garden railway, and more lines beyond. Many more. This is 'Britain's only 2ft *and* 2ft 6in dual-gauge railway'. In one of the engine sheds there's even a short stretch of standard line to accommodate engines that require 4ft 8in. And a half. Later that day I would lose count of the little engines chuffing about pulling carriages or just letting off steam, as if puffing out their cheeks like characters in a Reverend Awdry book. And in various immaculately maintained sheds there were yet more.

So who is Graham Lee? Well, he's the man behind Statfold Seed Oils, suppliers of flax, hemp, borage and the like for nutritional and personal care products. At harvest time, apparently, Statfold Barn becomes a working railway. Seed crops are transferred directly from combine harvester to a train of purpose-built bulk hopper wagons. He is also the chairman of LH Group Holdings of Burton-on-Trent, specialists in railway engineering, and in 2004 he negotiated the purchase of the Hunslet Engine Company of Leeds and its subsidiary, the Scottish company Andrew Barclay. Since the mid-19th century Hunslet had been responsible for building steam locomotives, including many narrow-gauge engines for the North Wales slate quarries. During World War I they had also built a number of narrow-gauge locos for the War Department for the little light railways supplying the trenches. In 1930 Hunslet had also acquired another locomotive maker, Kerr, Stuart & Co. Ltd, who'd been based not too far from Tamworth in Stoke-on-Trent and gone into liquidation. In 1995 Hunslet was still going, building little narrow-gauge diesel locomotives for use during the tunnelling for the Jubilee Line extension on the London Underground.

Eight years after buying Hunslet, Mr Lee sold the LH Group to Wabtec of Pittsburgh, Pennsylvania. Then he set up Hunslet Steam, the name used to distinguish the heritage aspects of Hunslet from its modern commercial operations under what is cosily called 'the Wabtec umbrella', a huge train-building operation that includes part of the former British Rail works in Doncaster. Those Hunslet Steam workshops here at Statfold Barn were helping to keep alight the flickering flame of British engineering skills. Apart from restoring locomotives and rolling stock built in various parts of the world, the team of around a dozen also built engines from scratch. Three since 2005, indeed, and all to traditional designs from Hunslet and Kerr, Stuart & Co.

It was obvious that I needed to talk to the somewhat elusive Mr Lee. I'd already been told he couldn't speak to me on the phone or arrange a specific meeting-point. So it was a matter of turning up and trying to truffle him out. Easier said than done. Despite the autumnal weather on this open day, there were an estimated *2,000* visitors.

Ah, here was somebody smartly dressed. Evidently an official of some sort. But no. He turned out to be a coach driver who had brought a large party from North Wales. 'All I'm looking for is a cup of tea,' he said. And every time I asked a police officer, engine driver, fireman or many another volunteer, the answer was usually the same: 'Graham? Oh, you've just missed him. He went that-a-way.'

Well, I went this-a-way and that-a-way but couldn't find him anyway. Perhaps it was time to climb aboard one of the many trains travelling around these expansive grounds and continue the search later. The one that would be setting off any time now from the main platform near the loco shed was to be pulled by an engine called *Saccharin*. Painstakingly restored and polished, it used to work on a sugar plantation in South Africa. Or so I was told by the fireman, who sported a splendid moustache and a cap worn at such a jaunty angle it was a wonder it managed to stay on once we were underway and he was leaning out of the cab at regular intervals. Perhaps he felt the need to cool off.

I felt the need to warm up, having given up my seat for one of the few ladies in a packed carriage and moved out to stand on a viewing ledge at the front, just behind the engine. The few other hardy souls out here were in anoraks and warm caps. Having mistakenly believed the weather forecaster who'd predicted that the Midlands would brighten up later, I'd come in an open-necked shirt topped by nothing more than a jacket with the collar turned up. Being closer to that boiler would have been an appealing option. It was full of Russian coal ('not as good as the Welsh'), which perhaps accounted for the darkness of the smoke belching from *Saccharin*'s funnel.

The carriage behind looked as appealing as the inside of a particularly expensive cigar box. Floor, ceiling and window frames were made of solid wood. So were the slatted seats, each with a polished brass knob on the top. Back out on the front ledge, meanwhile, one of the men in anoraks was telling his companion: 'I'm building a Yorkie, you know.'

With the ignorance of a long-ago trainspotter, I was about to ask what a Yorkie was when *Saccharin* let off an ear-splitting hoot that sent birds flapping skyward from the branches of distant trees. We were circumnavigating a huge field, ploughed in parts, with serious-looking photographers positioned along the line at regular intervals, huge umbrellas protecting those expensive cameras from the rain. In the middle distance – literally on the other side of the tracks – the grey sky was streaked with steam from other engines. Every now and then, one would pass us in the other direction, each packed to the rafters with passengers. There was a little green one called *Alpha*, originally from India, a little red one called *Fiji*, originally from... well, I'm sure I don't have to tell you, and then a black and red one. *Marylyn*, was it? No, *Marchlyn*.

Now here was an engine with a varied history. She had worked on the construction works at the Burnhope Reservoir in Weardale until 1936, when she was bought by Penrhyn Slate Quarries of North Wales. Somehow she had finished up on display at the Lake Winnepesaukah Amusement Park in Rossville, Georgia, until she was brought to Statfold Barn in 2011 and restored to full working order.

You could get off any train at Oak Tree Halt, wander into the nearby former grain store and get an even better sense of the sheer scale of the Lee family's collection. You climbed up a stairway on to a narrow balcony and gazed down on a dozen or so tracks radiating from a central turntable. No wonder the grain store has been re-christened 'the Roundhouse'. It wasn't as full of locos as usual today, of course, because so many of them were out on the tracks. But there were more than enough, some of them awaiting their turn to be transferred to the workshop. Or so I discovered later in the day. On this occasion I did the whole circuit in one go, keen as I was to meet the man behind this cornucopia of memorabilia.

'You haven't seen Graham Lee, have you?' I asked our jauntily be-capped fireman when we were back at the starting point and he had finally finished his duties in the cab.

'I saw him down the end of the platform a minute ago,' he replied. 'Looks as though he's gone now.'

Ah, well. Perhaps it was time to grab a word with our driver instead. Paul Ingham turned out to be a former college lecturer who normally worked on the Ffestiniog and Welsh Highland lines. 'I've been with the Ffestiniog since I was a young boy 46 years ago,' he told me.

'Doesn't it seem a bit flat to you here?'

'Yes, but nowhere else do you get the opportunity to drive such an eclectic mixture of locomotives; not only from South Africa and India but Indonesia, and Fiji. Then there are the ones that were built here, even if they had to be brought back from faraway places.' Java in the case of *Trangkil Number Four*, the last Hunslet steam train to be built at the Jack Lane Works in Leeds in 1971, three years after British Rail finally abandoned steam engines. Which might explain how it finished up on the Trangkil sugar mill estate in Java, where it worked for 30 years before being made redundant. It came home (well, almost) to Statfold Barn in 2004, where it was given a characteristically thorough overhaul and converted to a 2ft gauge.

My search for the man who bought it and brought it back began to warm up when I came across a young woman with a walkie-talkie who was dressed very differently from everyone else. It seemed quite a long way from the bottom of her well-fitting denim shorts to the top of her ankle boots. That space was filled by a pair of very evenly tanned legs. It came as no surprise to learn that Leanne Noon ran a beauty salon. What did surprise me was her reply to my question about what on earth she was doing here. 'Graham Lee,' she said, 'is my grandad-in-law.'

Bingo!

Yes, she'd seen him just a few minutes ago. And, unlike most, she could point me in his direction of travel. 'He's wearing a blue cap.' Well, that narrowed it down a bit. I strode off in the direction of a collection of large vans selling bacon rolls, burgers and much more, skirting round an enormous steam roller on one of the few open spaces without rails. Suddenly I spotted a blue cap. Beneath it was the still darkish hair of man unpretentiously clad in baggy jumper and jeans. Having just climbed into a small, mud-splattered van with a tabloid newspaper on the dashboard, he was about to set off when I leaned in and said: 'Mr Lee, I presume.'

'That's right.' The accent was Brummie but not broadly so. He seemed anxious to be off, so I congratulated him on attracting so many visitors on such a miserable day. 'Well, I'm 72 now and I've got a large collection of engines, I suppose. This is just a way of showing them off to other people who are interested, and raising a fair bit of money for local charities in the process.'

He had started this collection over 50 years ago, it transpired. 'It must have been around 1963.'

'In Birmingham?'

'Yes — although I came from Cradley Heath originally, from a family of Black Country metal-bashers. I've always been interested in Victorian engineering. These locos are mainly Victorian, and I suppose we've saved them from rotting away. There's about 12 on the team now doing full-time restoration.'

I was about to ask him a bit more about exactly how he got started, and how someone from a humble background had come so far. But he was already drumming his fingers on the dashboard. 'Got to move on,' he muttered. 'I'm looking for my dog at the moment. Black Labrador, in case you see it.' And with that he was off.

As I stepped away from the van, one of the steam-roller drivers was shouting, 'Mind your back. I'm doing a 14-point turn.' It was evidently time to beat a retreat, and go in search of the so-called Garden Railway.

Marchlyn back in her days at the Penrhyn Slate Quarries, 1957

The garden in question looked as though it might have been laid out by Capability Brown. There were even some small statues here and there. At the centre was a lake bordered by reeds, brushed by weeping willows and covered with water lilies. And round the edge, not of the lake but the whole garden, was a 2ft-wide railway line. That was something Capability could never have catered for, because he died long before the birth of the railways.

Circumnavigating the garden on that line today was *Howard*. Or was it *Hugo*? I was beginning to lose track, as it were. 'See that vertical boiler? It's like the ones they used on the Welsh slate quarries,' said Alan Glenister, a heavy goods vehicle driver from High

Wycombe with a very impressive camera. Come to think of it, *Howard* was standing nearby, with the address 'SOUTH ROAD, HOCKLEY BROOK, BIRMINGHAM' inscribed on its side in yellow capital letters. The carriages pulled by both trains were quite high above ground level. One poor man was putting his shoulder behind his wife's enormous bottom as he tried to heave her through the door. It didn't help that she seemed to be engulfed by giggles.

Having clambered into my carriage, Alan was snapping away happily, seemingly determined to capture every moment of the open day on film. 'You know what,' he proclaimed, sitting back in his seat and giving his camera a brief break: 'this has to be the best collection of narrow-gauge trains in the world!'

There was something surreal about chugging round such an elegant garden, being pulled by an engine that might once have transported slate from a quarry in North Wales. From the far side of the lake we had a slightly better view of what you might call Chateau Lee – the family home of the unassuming former 'Black Country metal basher' who built up this world-renowned collection from nothing. But the former farmhouse was fairly well shielded by trees, and all you could see was some weathered red brick and the glint of a glass roof that might have been a greenhouse or conservatory.

Leaping back to ground level again, I set off from the comparative peace and quiet of the garden to join a large crowd in the central courtyard outside the loco shed and workshop. Leanne's legs were easy to spot among the throng. As promised, she introduced me to her husband Nick, the man who now oversaw the building and restoration work that went on here on days when the public were not around. Most days, in other words. Yes, he confirmed, it was his grandad that encouraged his interest and, yes, he did his engineering apprenticeship at 16. He was now 29.

Was it difficult now to find trained engineers capable of doing this kind of work?

'It is, yes. Some of them are getting on a bit. I've had to make sure that I can do everything, so that I can supervise everything from cleaning the toilets to refurbishing an engine.'

'And do you have a favourite engine?'

'Probably *Fiji*, because it's between 60 and 70 per cent new. It was pretty well a wreck when it arrived here after many years of taking sugar to the coast and bringing coal back. Talking of coal, I "fired" her once' (he meant acted as fireman) 'all the way from Caernarfon to Porthmadog on the Welsh Highland line. I knew the manager there quite well. We do quite a bit of work here for other railways. In fact, we're doing some for the South Tynedale line at the moment.' That was on my list of railways to visit in due course.

Nick seemed like a good person to ask about the ongoing appeal of narrow-gauge railways. What was it about them that had attracted over 2,000 people on a chilly, wet autumnal day?

'With standard-gauge engines on the main lines, you can't really get close to them. But you can on these narrow-gauge lines. They're proper engines with lots of history.'

Quite a few Brummies of a certain age were reliving their own history in the workshops of their younger days. Some were almost dewy-eyed looking at the lathes, milling machines and grinders that have long gone from large parts of post-industrial Birmingham. Others were nodding knowledgeably and discussing the finer points of machinery that was always a mystery to me when I returned to the city during university vacations and did menial factory jobs to earn a few bob.

This visit to Statfold Barn seemed to be unearthing memories I'd long buried. Screwed to the walls of platforms were evocative adverts for products such as Allsop's Pale Ale, Sunlight Soap and Gold Flake cigarettes. Believe it or not, we used to collect cigarette packets as kids, usually from litter bins and pavements, cut out the fronts and stick them in scrapbooks. Gold Flake was a particularly cherished one of mine. Of course, I gave that up around the time I gave up trainspotting. I would have been 10 or 11. OK, 12 at the most.

In those days the 21st century belonged to the realms of science-fiction. It would have been hard to believe then that, in that century's second decade, so many men – and a few women – of my age and older would be flocking to somewhere near Tamworth to revel in steam-train travel that, by the end of the brave new world that was the 1960s, had already become ancient history.

10

THE LEGEND LOST FOR EVER

THE LEEK AND MANIFOLD VALLEY LIGHT RAILWAY

There is another part of Staffordshire, as different from the countryside around Tamworth as Northumberland is from Norfolk and Cumbria from Kentish marshland. The Moorlands are in the north of Staffs, partly inside the Peak District National Park, with the Pennines not far away. The landscape soars accordingly. Even on a grim and drizzly day, the short drive from Hulme End to Wetton Mill was distractingly scenic. It would have been a lot more enjoyable had I been on the Leek and Manifold Valley Light Railway, rather than at the wheel of a Ford Fiesta. Unfortunately, however, the L and MVLR closed rather a long time ago. In 1934, to be precise, 30 years after it opened.

I'd already discovered plenty of these strange little railways that had been brought back from the dead –

even completely rebuilt, in the case of the Welsh Highland, into a far more substantial undertaking than it had ever been in the beginning. And I'd just come from a network of narrow-gauge lines that was comparatively new. They hadn't been built to serve slate quarries or take tourists to see beautiful waterfalls, but because a man who liked trains had had the money to build a railway around his house and lay down more lines in the fields beyond.

Now I was in search of what you might call a narrow-gauge ghost, that had met its end around the same time as the Welsh Highland. Unlike the Welsh Highland, however, it had never made a comeback, except to haunt the memories of those who knew it, and the imagination of those who didn't.

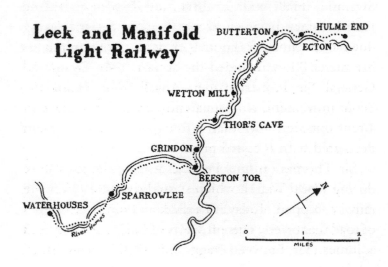

The stretch of road I was driving along would once have accommodated the trackbed. Indeed it didn't seem much wider than the original 2ft 6in gauge. Yes, of course it *was* wider but not wide enough to allow any vehicle coming the other way to carry on by without the roadway version of the passing loop. Lay-bys were few and far between but, mercifully, they materialised at the very moments when I encountered a postal van and a tractor. Having to back up on half a mile or so of narrow-gauge highway would have put a severe strain on the nerves and neck muscles. Particularly had I been in the 164yd long Swainsley Tunnel at the time.

The tunnel was built at the insistence of Sir Thomas Wardle, a local landowner. He was also a director of the railway, but didn't want it spoiling the view from Swainsley Hall, built in 1896, just two years before Parliamentary permission was granted for the laying down of the line. Sir Thomas evidently liked to impress his guests. They included the author Mark Twain and General Sir Robert Baden-Powell, founder of the Scout movement, who apparently preferred to sleep in a tent outside rather than a four-poster in a bedroom decorated with Rossetti prints.

Sir Thomas's tunnel became an ammunitions store during World War II, which started five years after the railway stopped. Today it's a dank and dimly-lit stretch of road that briefly cuts off views of the River Manifold as it meanders between craggy, almost cliff-like hillsides, frothing this way and that under the course of the old railway track.

At Wetton Mill the road swung sharply to the right while the trackbed carried straight on – well, as straight as any narrow-gauge line that has to negotiate the jutting lower slopes of steep hills. The former track was acquired by Staffordshire County Council from the LMS (London Midland and Scottish Railways) in 1937, tarmacked over and turned into a bridle path. Today it's known as the Manifold Way and is popular with cyclists. Walkers, too, judging by the number of booted and knapsacked couples I'd spotted striding forth with stout sticks.

By now you may be wondering why a light railway ever passed this way, and why it only lasted 30 years. The answer in both cases can be summed up in one word.

Milk.

There was a dairy and creamery at Ecton, the first of no fewer than nine registered calling points on the 8.25-mile journey from Hulme End to Waterhouses, and it evidently needed to get its prime product to a wider market – not least, perhaps, because there were a fair few dairy farms in the area that kept the locals well supplied. Judging by a short Pathé film, still viewable on YouTube, Ecton's milk was still being transported in churns as late as 1930. By that time there were tankers as well. But for much of the previous decade some 300 churns were unloaded daily at Waterhouses and transferred to mainline trains that ran daily – all the way to London.

Don't ask me why Londoners couldn't get milk supplies from closer to home. Nor indeed how it was kept chilled in the summer months. Maybe it was sterilised milk, very popular in the days when a fridge was regarded as a luxury by most families. Sterilisation was supposed to make milk last longer. 'Stera', as it was known, came with metal caps that had to be prised off with a bottle opener. My parents' neighbours were still having it delivered in the 1960s, and to me it tasted no better than sour milk.

Now, where were we?

Oh, yes, on the milk train south. According to Rebecca Simcock, who ran a tea room in the former engine shed at Hulme End, the 'churn-ey' from Ecton by narrow-gauge and main line finally came to a halt at Finsbury Park. From whence, presumably, liquid squeezed from the udders of North Staffordshire cows was transported to the doorsteps of North London.

Express Dairies closed their creamery at Ecton in 1932. The railway closed shortly afterwards as a direct consequence, only to reopen for a while the following year before shutting down for good in 1934. It was 10 March of that year, to be precise, and the last train had to plough through snow with very few passengers on board. The line had always carried passengers as well as milk, but the population in these parts was, and still is, thinly spread. Bank holidays apart, churns greatly outnumbered members of the travelling public.

Rebecca's Tea Junction was closed for the winter months, but she had kindly agreed to open up and show me where she now served Bakewell tart, Victoria sponge, lemon drizzle and other home-made delights. And the milk for the tea?

'That comes from Buxton Dairies, just up the road.' She pointed out two of the original metal beams supporting the curved roof of the former engine shed. The rest was rebuilt by the local council a hundred years or so after it first opened, in the style and brown and yellowy-cream colours of the railway.

Around it were other reminders of the railway's Edwardian origins, including a timetable for 29 June 1904. There was a large sign informing visitors that this was Hulme End and to change here for Sheen and Hartington. Original sleepers from the railway had been re-laid either side of the main doors and, to the right, were platform benches: one for Hulme End and the other for the station at Thor's Cave. I would get a glimpse of that cave later in the day – an expansive hole in a steep limestone crag, named after a Norse god. Excavations have showed that it was occupied some 10,000 years ago.

The ticket office at Hulme End was occupied somewhat more recently, and part of it was still there. Rebecca found the key, opened it up and pointed out the original glass hatch. Then she opened up another

E.R. Calthrop *at Waterhouses, 1937*

Side view of E.R. Calthrop *at Waterhouses, 1937*

door to reveal the original wooden panelling and original fireplace, albeit with a somewhat more modern log-effect gas fire fronting it.

'Still, it has a real railway feel about this place,' I pointed out.

Rebecca sniffed the mustiness with evident distaste. 'Bit of a smell about it, too.'

Tickets purchased here would have secured passengers a place on one of four coaches (two first-class, two third) painted originally in a somewhat startling primrose yellow. Until the LMS took over in 1923, that is, and slapped on the corporate maroon. As for the two engines, decked out in brown and gold, they were painted black, as if to predict the railway's eventual demise.

One engine was named *J.R.Earle*, after the resident engineer, the other *E.R.Calthrop* in honour of the engineer brought in to oversee the design and layout of the whole line. Calthrop had built the Barsi Light Railway in India, which may explain the somewhat colonial aspect of the engines. They had large headlights, which were never used, and fitments for cow catchers, which were never fitted. As for the railway track itself, this was fitted to such a high standard that the rails never had to be re-laid. Those engines must have been top-quality too. Unlike those on any other narrow-gauge line in this country, they sometimes had to pull heavily laden standard-gauge milk and coal wagons into sidings along the way.

Once they were finally ripped up, Calthrop's well-laid rails were never replaced. An attempt in the 1970s to revive part of the line between Grindon and Wetton came to nothing. Ramblers protested that the valley was already too congested during the summer months. One apparently suggested that Blackpool might be a better location for such a venture.

Probably a descendent of Sir Thomas Wardle, I was thinking to myself as the end of the Swainsley Tunnel came in sight. Wetton Mill came in sight, too. Eventually. It was tucked away over a small stone bridge and under a huge jutting crag that evidently contained another cave. Old Hannah's Hole, this one was called. Presumably old Hannah was somewhat more local than Thor.

They used to grind corn at the mill. Now it housed another tea room, also closed for the winter, and also run by another obliging local lady who was prepared to open the place up and show me around. In fact, Jeannette Mellor did more than that. She drove me all the way over the other side of the valley in her enormous 4x4 Toyota that somehow fitted into these narrow lanes in the way that, I imagined, standard-gauge wagons once squeezed into narrow-gauge sidings along that long-defunct line. Our destination was Waterhouses, at the southern end of the line. And, no, we didn't meet a single vehicle coming the other way.

'There used to be a copper mine up here,' Jeannette was saying. The owner had a road bridge built to

Train at Hulme End c.1904

connect with the railway. But they didn't lay the line as quickly as he expected once permission was granted, and the mine went bust in the meantime. In fact, the Ecton Mine had peaked about a century previously, and it's remarkable that it lasted as long as it did.

As we arrived in Waterhouses, Jeannette pointed out some old railway cottages before veering off the road, up a slope and parking outside the handsomely restored former goods shed. These days it housed bikes rather than trains. Bikes for hire and bikes for sale. Closed for the winter – surprise, surprise, but the owners of the few cars hereabouts still had to make sure they had purchased a parking ticket.'Have you paid and displayed?' enquired a large blue sign 200 yards or so beyond the shed where the former trackbed disappeared into the trees. 'Apparently, people used to ride their bikes over the sleepers in the days after the railway closed and before the Council laid down the tarmac,' said Jeannette, who grew up on a nearby dairy farm.

'My grandad used to walk to the end of one of the fields when he needed to go to Hulme End. It wasn't one of the halts, but the train driver would pull up anyway. What's more, he'd drop him off in exactly the same place on the way back. We had a lady who used to come into the Mill tea rooms,' she went on to recall, 'who told me that she travelled on it regularly to go and see relatives in Hulme End. And she lived in Leek.'

That would have meant starting on the main line (or a trolley bus) before boarding the narrow-gauge railway at Waterhouses.

Leek hasn't had a station of any kind since 1970, and passenger trains stopped running there five years previously. More's the pity, I muttered to myself as I drove round and round the town looking for a parking space. A branch of Morrisons now stands on the site, and the nearest you'll get to the original station is a picture on the wall in Julie's on Derby Street – yet another tea room, but at least this one was open.

Admittedly, there is a Leek Brook Station on the Churnet Valley, a preserved standard-gauge railway. And the Moorlands District Council has finally given planning permission for a quarter-mile extension that could see that line eventually terminate on an industrial estate in the town itself.

The Leek and Manifold line, meanwhile, appeared to have terminated for good. For the foreseeable future the former trackbed was going to remain the province of walkers, cyclists and, for a few miles at least, drivers with steady nerves and flexible necks.

11

RETURN TICKET
TO RED SQUIRRELS

The Ravenglass and Eskdale Light Railway

My mainline train from Lancaster stopped briefly at Carnforth. A *Brief Encounter*, you might say, because it was here in north Lancashire rather than the Home Counties that the great director David Lean came in 1945 to shoot the location scenes for that most English of films. Celia Johnson and Trevor Howard came with him, needless to say. Apart from a cameo appearance by Stanley Holloway, the other stars were the trains. Noel Coward's screenplay explored the sexual repression of the times, and Lean made the most of those thrusting pistons and the all-pervasive steaminess.

When I first visited Carnforth in the 1990s, it had just been voted the worst station in Britain. Cracks in the platforms were sprouting knee-high weeds, and the underpass where Celia's 'heppily married' Laura kissed Alec (Trevor in a trilby) was now a murky and mildewed

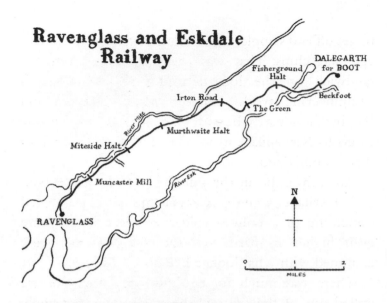

Ravenglass and Eskdale Railway

DALEGARTH for BOOT
Fisherground Halt
Irton Road
Beckfoot
The Green
Murthwaite Halt
Miteside Halt
River Mite
Muncaster Mill
River Esk
RAVENGLASS

N

0   1   2
MILES

dungeon. Slivers of peeling paintwork shivered as expresses thundered overhead.

Enter the Carnforth Station and Railway Trust, to restore the long-since derelict Refreshment Room and make it look much as it did in the movie, complete with silver tea urns and a till that rang up the takings in shillings and pence. Mind you, when I went back to Carnforth about six years after my first visit, I couldn't get so much as a rock cake to eat. 'It's the rationing,' one of the volunteers had smiled. So I'd gone next door to another beautifully restored former station building, where *Brief Encounter* was showing on a loop, and then called in at a nearby branch of Greggs for a cheese and onion pasty. Since then, it seems, a full lunch menu has materialised. But I can't say that I was tempted to get off and sample, say, the Cumberland sausage with egg and chips. That was partly because I'd had a sandwich on the long-delayed Virgin train north ('Engineering works between Milton Keynes and Rugby'), and partly because there was still a long way to go to Ravenglass, in what is now Cumbria rather than Cumberland.

Apart from the area around the Refreshment Room and 'Heritage Centre', Carnforth Station remained something of a railway wilderness. The weeds were even higher in parts, and the many sidings were crammed with what looked like disused diesels.

There was much to see, however, soon after we pulled out of the station. The train was surprisingly crowded, but luckily my view was only slightly obscured by the woman sitting opposite, who had climbed aboard at the last minute and was sharing her seat with a knapsack almost as big as herself. Across the gangway to the left sat another woman seemingly gripped by a story in her magazine and oblivious to the glories of Morecambe Bay unfolding through the panoramic window beyond her. Flat sands and shimmering pools stretched away to a horizon where distant cliffs and hills seemed to converge with banks of fluffy cloud.

The bay is famous for its shellfish as well as its views. But the deaths of 23 Chinese cockle-pickers in 2004 were a jolting reminder that you have to know where not to go out there, and beware of those sudden

Miteside railway station, 1903

Northern Rock *at Eskdale Green, 1976*

incoming tides. Yet from a train window it looked so
calm and peaceful. Even when the tide comes in, I
remembered somebody at Carnforth telling me, passing
over the Arnside Viaduct is 'like being in an ocean-
going liner'. At least the slightly lower waters this
afternoon allowed a glimpse of that magnificent piece
of railway architecture, restored by Network Rail
in 2011.

We stopped at many a station, every one more
attractive than Carnforth. Perhaps the most memorable
was Grange-over-Sands, with its handsome buildings
of solid stone, its Victorian lamp posts and its glass
canopies supported by ornate iron-work. Not forgetting
the view of the town's promenade overlooking the bay
as the train swung through a sharp bend to the left and
followed the coastline.

Barrow-in-Furness was always better known for
its ship-building than its railway, but it was there that
those of us heading even further north had to change
and wait for the 14.37. I'm sure Barrow has its
picturesque parts, but they weren't too evident from
the somewhat ancient train conveying us onwards and
upward. Normal service was soon resumed, however.
More wide expanses of marshland, sand and sea to the
left, more steep green slopes worthy of a Lakeland
Crayons tin to the right. It went on like that most of
the way to Ravenglass. When I finally disembarked at
the mainline station, I felt rather as I had in North
Wales: totally 'scened' out. Perhaps dashing across to the

narrow-gauge line next door to catch the last train to Dalegarth wouldn't be such a good idea.

Although they were at opposite ends of the country, the narrow-gauge railway here had always had a close relationship with the Romney, Hythe and Dymchurch down in Kent. With a gauge of just 15 inches they were both small, even by narrow-gauge standards, and they were therefore able to lend each other engines every now and then. Mind you, only the Ravenglass and Eskdale line is known as the 'La'al Ratty' – Cumbrian dialect, as you may have gathered. 'La'al' is 'little'. And 'Ratty'? That's short for 'rat track' or 'rat run' – a rather uncomplimentary term for what was trailed as one of the most scenic railway journeys in England. Then again, it may just be a reflection of size. Most adults could stand by the side of one of these engines or carriages and look down on them.

Apart from anything else, waiting for the first train out the next morning gave me the chance of a chat with Peter Van Zeller. He'd been working here since 1968, and driving steam trains full-time since 1973. Professionally, that is. The Ravenglass and Eskdale has well over 50 active volunteers out of a worldwide membership not far short of 17,000, but the steam train drivers tend to be either old pros as in Peter's case (he was 67) or young pros like Will Sande, 26, whom I would meet later.

For the time being, Peter and I were sitting outside the narrow-gauge station cafe with a cup of tea and, in my case, a piece of cappuccino cake. Luckily, I'd just finished it when the station cat leapt on to the table, strolled between us without so much as a by-your-leave, and started hoovering up the crumbs. Sorry, Peter, you were saying?

'Despite having a Dutch name, I've lived in this area all my life, and the Ravenglass and Eskdale offered the chance to do what I'm still doing now.'

'And still enjoying it?'

'It's a way of life. You're conscious of being part of the scenery but, beyond the track, that scenery changes every day. You might see a buzzard one minute and a herd of red deer the next. But it's also a challenge. If you get it wrong or the weather changes, the terrain can be against you. Not for a minute can you let your guard down.' Sheep could run on to the line, needless to say. And rocks could occasionally fall and roll on to it. He shrugged. 'These things happen.'

Not that the La'al Ratty has always had a gauge of 15 inches. The original railway's track was more than twice that width when it opened in 1875 to transport iron ore from the mines above the village of Boot, near Scafell, to the mainline station at Ravenglass, some 7 miles away. Passengers were allowed to travel the following year. Not enough of them, it seems, found the prospect of being conveyed up and down the line in goods wagons too appealing. In 1897 the line was declared bankrupt, but somehow it kept going until April 1913, by which time the bottom had dropped out of the iron-ore market with a resounding clang.

Two model-makers with expansive pockets as well as names, Wenman Joseph Bassett-Lowke and Robert Proctor-Mitchell, acquired the line in 1915. They spent the next two years converting it to the current 15in gauge. Not just for their own pleasure, it must be said, nor solely for the pleasure of others. Apart from passengers, trains also conveyed granite from Beckfoot Quarry to the Murthwaite crushing plant. Passenger traffic was suspended during World War II, and by 1948 the line had been bought by the Keswick Granite Company. Quarrying ceased at Beckfoot in 1953, but the line was saved from closure by the Ravenglass and Eskdale Railway Preservation Society, which bought it from the granite company in 1960.

The following year the Society made a very astute appointment. One Douglas Ferreira became general manager and stayed in that post until 1994, transforming the line into a major tourist attraction in an area not short of attractions. It helped, perhaps, that passengers no longer had to travel in goods wagons, where they must have had a somewhat limited view of the sort of countryside that the fell-walking author and illustrator Alfred Wainwright immortalised.

Today you have a choice of carriages: either open to elements or offering the chance to batten down the hatches when the weather is inclement. We passed a line of them as Peter showed me the sheds where venerable engines were gleaming in the gloom. There was *Typhoon*, on loan from the Romney, Hythe and Dymchurch. 'It'll be on a lorry heading south again soon,' he assured me, 'once *Northern Rock* comes out of the workshop.'

Hmm... the name sounded familiar. And, no, not because of the former building society of the same name. Ah, yes, that was it. We'd been pulled by an engine called *Northern Chief* on the R, H and D to Dungeness in the far southeast of England. Elements of the *Chief*, it turned out, had been incorporated into the *Rock* when it was designed by Ian Smith, the then chief engineer at Ravenglass, in the 1970s. He also used some of the design aspects of *River Irt* which, having done its duty for yet another day, was parked a little way outside ready to head for the shed.

Now here was an engine with some history. She was called *Muriel* when she came into being in 1894 at Duffield Bank in Derbyshire. After the death of her designer, Sir Arthur Heywood, she was requisitioned for war work at the Gretna Munitions Factory. Somehow she found her way back over the English border the following year and finished up at Ravenglass. Ten years later she acquired a new boiler, a new cab, an extended frame and a new name. But as *River Irt* she remained the oldest 15in-gauge engine in the world

Ninety years on and she looked as good as new. Take it from one who climbed aboard that cab and travelled at least a hundred yards, albeit backwards towards the shed. At the helm was the aforesaid Will Sande, who had just done the last trip up the line. For today at least. 'I still have a lot of polishing to do before knocking off,' he said.

Really? It looked handsomely polished already. Even the coal behind us appeared almost impossibly shiny. And, no, it wasn't Welsh opencast coal. 'German anthracite,' Will revealed. 'It gives a comparatively clean smoke. A fair bit of heat as well.' Not that it was too hot here in the cab; just pleasantly warm.

Will turned out to have a degree in microbiology from the University of the West of England in Bristol. So what was he doing driving a train?

'I've been coming here all my life. My dad was at school with Peter, and I must have been about four months when he first brought me here. I started volunteering in 2008, and it struck me that this was what I wanted to do. It's quite special, and I feel privileged to be part of it.'

'So what's the appeal of narrow-gauge?'

'It's going back in time, really. These engines are very hardy and very manageable. Yes, we do long hours. In summer it's 12 hours a day, but even on cold, wet days you're close up to ethereal views, and it's even better on hot days because you don't get much smoke.'

Well, tomorrow I was going to see those ethereal views close up. Without any smoke, what's more. But for now it was time to check out the views at the Ravenglass end of the line, starting with a World

Beckfoot Station in 1906, in the days before the line was converted to 15in gauge

Heritage Site. The Roman bathhouse was not much more than half a mile's walk from the station along a pleasant, tree-lined path. Not exactly Pompeii, but an impressive reminder all the same of the ancient history of this, the only coastal village in the Lake District National Park. While the fort that once surrounded the bathhouse might have gone, the walls had survived remarkably well. They were over 8ft high in parts, and you could walk under an arch while trying to imagine the sights and smells of another golden age of steam that had existed here some two thousand years ago.

Back on the station bridge, the sun was beginning to go down behind the yard arm. Time for a pint, perhaps. The centre of Ravenglass was only a few minutes' walk away. If anybody decided to make a better film of *Under Milk Wood* than the last one, this could have been the setting for Llareggub. No, it wasn't Wales, any more than Carnforth is the Home Counties. That doesn't matter when it comes to making movies. What matters is that Ravenglass had an evocative main street leading, at either end, to the sort of harbour that Captain Cat could dream of setting sail from once more.

It looked even better when I finally sat down outside the Inn at Ravenglass and sampled the Yates Bitter, brewed not too far from here. The tide was out, and the few boats languishing in the sand looked as though they might have been marooned for weeks. But the sunset provided a spectacular backdrop that could have graced any film, be it *Under Milk Wood* or a promotional video by the Cumbria Tourist Board. Not only was the sun lighting up the clouds with a deep ruddy glow, it was also casting beams of light on to the few flat mirrors of water below.

'Not much fishing goes on these days,' I was told by the man on an adjoining table – an engineer, it turned out, briefly back home in Ravenglass after weeks of working in Antarctica. 'The razor fish are shipped over to Ireland en route to Japan, but you sometimes get a lobster or two on the menus round here.'

Not at this pub. Not tonight, anyway. Nor did they have a spare table for one. 'We've got a party coming in later,' I was curtly informed. Ah, well. The Ratty Arms it was, then. No spectacular views here at the back of the station, but the charming Chinese barmaid provided a warm welcome. She even offered to wrap up the remains of the mountain of meat that came with my shank of lamb. I declined on the grounds that (a) I didn't have a dog and (b) I was staying overnight in a former first-class Pullman carriage parked nearby.

You could rent the *Maid of Kent* for a week. She was one of two Edwardian-style 'camping coaches' side by side next to the narrow-gauge line. Plenty of polished dark wood, I'd noticed when I'd dropped off my bag earlier. There was also a little kitchen with a fridge and cooker, a living/dining area with a table, a telly and a comfortable Pullman double seat. Beyond was a lengthy corridor, past a compartment or two with bunk beds for the kids, to another room with a couple of what might be called narrow-gauge beds and a shower room with a WC. Thankfully, there was no sign telling you not to flush it while standing in the station.

It was broad daylight when I'd first seen it. When I emerged from the Ratty Arms, however, it was 'a moonless night in the small town, starless and bible black', as the Dylan who never won the Nobel Prize for Literature would have put it. A torch would have been a blessing. The beginning of the Ravenglass and Eskdale line looked rather different when you couldn't see your hand in front of your face. In fact, it looked like nothing at all. But somehow I managed to grope, stumble and fumble my way home. And, no, I wasn't the worse for wear. Being finally reunited with the *Maid of Kent* was something of a relief, until I turned on the telly and *Aaaaaaagh!* There was Michael Portillo on one of his *Great Continental Railway Journeys*. He was in Morocco. Even tried to do an impression of Humphrey Bogart in *Casablanca*. Suddenly it seemed rather a long time since my most recent brief encounter with Carnforth Station.

In the morning sunlight Ravenglass narrow-gauge station had been restored to an attractive departure point. Hanging baskets still bloomed in early October, and a red telephone box offset the blue and white of the carriages. Sweeping them out shortly before taking up guard duties on the 9.25 departure was volunteer Simon Garrod, who once had the somewhat more taxing responsibility of being health and safety manager at the Sellafield nuclear power station. 'I took my girlfriend on this train in 1975 and we're still married,' he beamed. She obviously liked it.

Now here I was with a grandstand view from the cab of the *Douglas Ferreira*, a diesel named after the venerable former manager. At the helm, as I waved goodbye to the *Maid of Kent*, was Jackie Pharaoh, who had first indulged her love of trains on the Bressingham steam line, just over the border from her native Suffolk. 'My husband comes from up this way, so I started driving here when I retired from my job as a medical secretary,' she told me shortly before a suicidal pheasant skimmed across the front screen, narrowly escaping a splattering.

What did I say about nature red in tooth and claw?

'There's a red squirrel,' Jackie casually observed, gesturing to the right. Yes, I saw it! Bit of a blur, mind you, as it shot between the pines and birches in a wood seemingly ablaze with golden bracken. Now, I've seen more than enough grey squirrels. Used to be plagued by the damn things in the days when the kids were at home, the house was bedlam and I used to write in a shed. But this was my first sighting of that much-persecuted native British species.

'There's a buzzard,' Jackie gestured to the left this time. Damn. I must have just missed it. There was so much to take in. The estuary at Ravenglass, which we'd glimpsed soon after pulling out, already seemed like a distant memory. We were climbing now up a gradient of 1 in 50, and the skyline seemed to be full of fells. Soon after pulling out of Miteside Halt, with its delightful platform seat like a vertical hammock for two, Muncaster Fell came into view to the right – a great green and craggy ridge of majestic proportions. Then, soon after we passed the remains of the plant that used to crush all that granite, there to the left was the more pointed Irton Fell, rising to nearly 1,300ft. And that was nothing. Straight ahead was a glimpse of Scafell thrusting through fluffy clouds to a height of over 3,000ft.

By now the gradient had increased to 1 in 40 as we turned through a sharp right-hand bend around some jutting rocks. Down to the left, the tops of trees were lit up by a beaming sun. The golden leaves and bracken by the side of the line stirred in the breeze as we passed. We'd gone by several halts with no passengers waiting to board. Until we reached The Green, that is, to be waved down by a couple who were just about to climb aboard when one of them rushed back to their camper van to pick up an umbrella. Well, you can never be too sure about the weather in the northwest. Jackie waited patiently. Had I but world enough and time, I would have got off to explore the beauties of Eskdale, especially as Simon the guard had told me that there was a stunning cricket pitch hereabouts.

But the couple were now on the train and we were off, passing under a handsomely proportioned stone bridge built in the days of the 3ft gauge. There were dry-stone walls and sheep galore either side. Suddenly two of them were on the line. In fact, they were running backwards and forwards across it for a distance of half a mile or so, seemingly oblivious to blasts on the hooter, until they finally disappeared on a sharp bend to the left. 'The red deer are worse,' Jackie confided. 'They'll just run at you. It can be quite scary sometimes.'

There were no deer today, on the line or off it, from what I could see. No Clydesdale horses either. 'I had one standing under a bridge once and refusing to budge,' Jackie went on. 'Well, I can cope with sheep, but I don't do horses. Luckily there was a lady on the train who did. She finally managed to lure him off the line and into a field.'

Not surprisingly, the railway's mining and quarrying past became slightly more evident towards the top end of the line. There was even a row of former miners' cottages, almost every one now with a satellite dish attached.

Cumbria may be one of the most hauntingly beautiful counties in England, but here and elsewhere it harbours a rich mining past. Force Crag at the head of the Coledale Valley was the last lead mine in the Lake District. It opened in the 1880s and had a brief revival a century later when they were drilling for barite (used in hospital barium meals, among other things) rather than lead.

There were coal mines on the far west coast of Cumbria, burrowing miles out to sea under the Solway Firth. Most were named after World War I generals and, like their namesakes, they were responsible for many deaths. Not from sea water surging in, but from methane gas that seeped into the nostrils and turned their tunnels and seams into potentially explosive traps.

The Ravenglass line had served the iron-ore mine above Boot and, believe me, in the 19th and early 20th centuries Cumbria was riddled with iron ore mines. There had been well over 200 within a 12-mile radius of here. Like the reddleman in Thomas Hardy's *The Return of the Native*, miners would emerge at the end of a shift covered in red dust (albeit for different reasons) and have to walk home to have it washed off their clothes and skin. Quite a few of them had been of Irish descent, their ancestors having crossed 'the water' in some numbers after the potato famine of the 1840s, and pale-faced Catholics must have felt uncomfortably like Orange men at times.

There were Scottish immigrants as well. Italians, too. It could be a combustible mixture when they gathered for a drink after work. Or so I recall two former miners telling me with knowing chuckles when I'd met them about four years earlier at an iron ore mine just up the coast at Egremont, about 12 miles northwest of Ravenglass. Although well into their 70s, they were still flogging an occasional 60 tons or so of ore to a Swedish company. There was a great pile of the stuff in the yard behind the long-closed mine where they once worked, and where they now ran a small business from a time-warp of an office. That ore was as red as the sunset I'd marvelled at far more recently while gazing out over the estuary at Ravenglass. Not anywhere near as mesmerising, mind you.

Here at the far end of this narrow-gauge line, not for the first time in the course of these narrow-gauge travels, I found myself marvelling at how the strain, stress, turbulence and misery of our mining past had somehow been enfolded back into the landscape, leaving hardly a scar behind.

As I stepped out of Dalegarth Station, there was the unsullied countryside that had set the Wainwright pen and paintbrush flowing. Walks galore beckoned. About half a mile up the road to the right, I found myself standing on a stone bridge, mesmerised by a fast-flowing river bubbling around the rocks below. A little gateway and path to the right led to St Catherine's Church, a compact blend of stone and stained glass dwarfed by a backdrop of Scafell Pike, the highest mountain in England. Stanley Ghyll Waterfall isn't that high but, by God, it looked spectacular as it cascaded down the rock face up beyond the bridge and plunged into the river below.

It was still dry and bright when it became time for the journey back, so I sat in one of the open-air carriages. Nearby was a man with binoculars almost welded to his eyes the whole way. You didn't need them to catch occasional glimpses of that gleaming diesel engine as it wound round bends and the sun beamed down on its pristine paintwork.

At Irton Road loop we were passed by another diesel with another female driver. And there was Peter in the cab with her. We passengers in the open-topped carriages didn't just wave at one another; we passed the time of day.

'Morning.'

'Morning.'

And so on until we parted company.

Back at Ravenglass, Morecambe Bay beckoned, followed eventually by the somewhat more mundane sights of Wigan, Warrington and Wolverhampton on the lengthy Virgin Trains journey south from Lancaster. But first of all I had a quick chat with binocular-man. He was from Sittingbourne in Kent.

'Funny you should mention that. I was on the Sittingbourne and Kemsley line a few months ago,' I said, before stating the obvious: 'Very different from this.'

'Yes, the scenery here is quite stunning. Mind you, I'm very disappointed that I haven't seen a red squirrel.'

'Ah. Funny you should mention that…'

12

A VISION OF A
TOWN REBORN

The South Tynedale Railway

It was a memorable Monday morning. While much of the world had begun the working week in lengthy traffic jams or on crowded buses, trains and tubes, I'd been driven across spectacular scenery in one of the most remote parts of the UK. Shafts of sunlight would suddenly slice through clouds shrouding the tops of hills on which nothing much grew nor grazed. A rainbow had peeped over the ridge of the North Pennines. And ahead the road wound this way and that as my ears popped and we passed a couple of masochistic cyclists. There was no other traffic.

Then we'd begun our descent towards Alston. Yes, that's right: our *descent*. Alston may be the highest market town in England – well over 1,000ft above sea level at its peak – but Alston Moor is even higher. We were still in Cumbria (just about), but far east of

Ravenglass and the west coast, and heading for Northumberland. By train, once we'd parked outside the Alston end of the South Tynedale Railway. The county border was not far away, which was just as well, as the South Tynedale only went about 3.5 miles to Lintley Halt. So far.

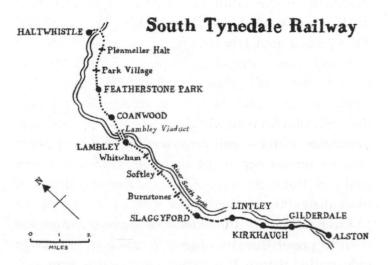

South Tynedale Railway

HALTWHISTLE
Plenmeller Halt
Park Village
FEATHERSTONE PARK
COANWOOD
Lambley Viaduct
LAMBLEY
Whitwham
Softley
Burnstones
SLAGGYFORD
LINTLEY
KIRKHAUGH
GILDERDALE
ALSTON
River South Tyne
N
0 1 2
MILES

This was another kind of narrow-gauge line altogether. There had been a railway in the town since the late 19th century, built, once again, to serve the mines (lead and coal, in this case) – but it had been your standard-gauge variety. Whistles still blow at regular intervals after mainline trains en route between Newcastle and Carlisle have come to a halt at Haltwhistle, where the Alston branch had terminated. A good name for a station if ever there was one. But despite surviving the Beeching cuts of the previous decade, the branch line to Alston was closed in 1976.

'The reason this line lasted so long was that it was the only reliable means of transport to Alston at the height of the winter,' Stuart Hines, the railway manager of the South Tynedale Railway told me over a mean Americano in the station cafe. 'Sure enough, the winter of 1976 was so harsh that all the roads were closed and Alston was completely cut off.'

Stuart came originally from Suffolk. The lady behind the cafe counter was from Essex. The mechanical engineer she was just serving had driven a mere 50 miles from Newcastle, as he did every morning, sometimes with his springer spaniel for company. Steve Hopper turned out to be one of comparatively few paid staff. But there were over 50 active volunteers and more than 400 members nationwide.

Originally, after the branch closed, the plan had been to preserve and reopen it as it was as a heritage railway. But British Rail asked for a lot more money than the Preservation Society could then afford, and consequently pulled up all the track. So the decision was taken to start again from the Alston end, re-laying it as a narrower gauge railway and therefore lighter on cost. Today's South Tynedale Railway members were united in the conviction that the Haltwhistle connection – a further 10 miles or so beyond Lintley – would become a reality one day, albeit in a 2ft rather than a 4ft 8½in gauge.

That long-term dream came a little closer to reality when in 2014 the National Heritage Lottery Fund awarded the Preservation Society a grant of £4 million. 'A lifeline for the railway,' Stuart called it. With that, they could rebuild the platform opposite and the canopy that once linked both platforms – in glass and wrought iron rather than the original corrugated rust. And, more importantly, perhaps, they could extend the line just over a mile beyond Lintley to the village of Slaggyford. 'All the drainage and maintenance work has been done by our volunteers,' said Stuart. 'We're bringing in contractors to lay down the track. Then we've got to install a car park so that people from Slaggyford will have a park-and-ride facility if they want to go shopping in Alston.'

The economic benefits for Alston of the whole long-term project could be discussed later. For now it was time to leave the cafe with its British Rail posters evoking the joys of Whitley Bay and Berwick-upon-Tweed. The first train of the day was waiting outside. It was also the first day of the October half-term, so the platform was thronged with excited children, many of them clutching colouring sheets provided with their tickets.

The railway's rolling stock was an eclectic mix, to put it mildly. The steam engines included *Barber*, a one-time veteran of the Harrogate Gas Works line, and a 1934 Hunslet called *Green Dragon* that had run for many years on a sugar plantation in South Africa. Then there were two battery-driven maintenance locos from the London Underground. But pulling us on the 10.45 today was an old stalwart from closer to home. *Naworth* was a diesel that shunted trucks about in one of the many mines that once warrened the landscape hereabouts. The carriages into which we'd just piled were also local. Built by an engineering company in Alston, I was told. And to a high standard, judging by the red padded seats and coordinating carpet in here. Not to mention the light wooden tables and matching luggage racks.

It seemed doubtful that five-year-old Millie Lawson had noticed the surroundings. She was colouring frantically while sitting on her mother's knee at the table across the gangway. 'We've been coming on this line since Josh was in his Thomas the Tank Engine phase,' said Kimberley Lawson. 'He's 10 now.' The Josh in question was her son, needless to say, and he was sitting behind us with his grandparents. From a quick glance, he looked older than 10 and intelligent enough to be reading Tolstoy rather than Thomas in the not-too-distant future.

'I loved trains when I was a kid. Still do, I suppose,' his father Doug was saying in a voice that wouldn't have sounded out of place on the 8.15 from Sunbury-on-Thames to Waterloo. He ran a team of software consultants, and had moved the family from Sunbury to Penrith a few years earlier. 'It was there or Reading, and I haven't regretted it. We even saw the *Flying Scotsman* on the Settle–Carlisle line not long ago.'

As the far-from-flying 10.45 eased out of Alston, an unusual Monday morning became slightly surreal, as we rolled past a stall selling 'Artisan Crêpes'. *Sacré bleu!* Was this northern England or northern France; Britain or Brittany? Within 50yds or so of the crêpe stall, a bearded volunteer in a yellow jacket was standing outside the signal box, beaming happily and waving to the children. He would turn out to be an Emeritus Professor from Edge Hill University in Ormskirk.

There would be time for a chat with him on our return. Maybe, too, a closer look at that line of trams just beyond the box on the right-hand side of the line. They came originally from Vienna, according to Stuart, and had been built in the 1950s. 'They'd lain derelict at a railway company in Romania for years. We heard about them through a contact and persuaded the Romanians to re-gauge them for us, from 2ft 6in to 2ft, and ship them over here.'

'Must have been cheaper than having the work done locally?'

'Much.'

We were travelling at not much more than 12 miles per hour but, all the same, the border with Northumberland had been upon us as soon as we'd crossed the Gilderdale Viaduct. Not that there had been much change in the scenery. The South Tynedale River continued to meander this way and that, flowing under the line at various points and reappearing through the right- or the left-hand window. Wooded banks were bathed in autumnal russet, tinged with gold every now and then as occasional shafts of sunlight pierced the cloud. Then the trees would break up to reveal swathes of moorland with wildlife in abundance. Here a hare bounding across clumps of lumpy grass; there a pheasant perched on a dry-stone wall.

My appreciation of the bird life along the line was enhanced by my chauffeur for the day, Mick Botterill, an old mate and a former biology teacher, who'd driven me over from his home in Kirkby Stephen and come along for the ride. 'See those mallards taking off from that boggy patch over there?' he'd say.

To be honest, I'd thought that they were pigeons, or maybe gulls.

'Look at all those grouse rushing up the hill.'

It was like being with Will Grundy, the gamekeeper in *The Archers*. Any minute now I half expected the local version of Brian Aldridge and his green-wellied chums to appear and start blasting their shotguns. But all remained peaceful out there, and the only thing spooking those grouse appeared to be the rumble of our train as it trundled past.

'There's a buzzard,' said Mick casually. And this time I didn't miss it, as I had done on the Ravenglass line across the county border. There it was, hovering on the horizon, in all its wide-winged menace. Thanks, Mick.

One item of wildlife I had yet to clap eyes on, here or on the Ravenglass line, was a deer. Quite plentiful in these parts, I'd been told. But they didn't appear to be venturing anywhere near the train today. At least there were some deer-like sculptures, carved in a reddish sort of wood, on the platform at Kirkhaugh, the only stop on the South Tynedale line apart from Lintley – although Slaggyford will probably be open by the time you read this. At Kirkhaugh a small party disembarked, clad in boots and anoraks, knapsacks on their backs and taut leads tugging on their fingers. Their dogs evidently wanted to be off. Whether they wanted to visit the ruins of the fort known as Epiacum, once the gateway to the Roman Empire in Northumberland, was debatable. But their owners may well have had that in mind. Well worth the walk, I was told, for those suitably booted.

Those of us still on the train passed under another handsome stone bridge. There were no fewer than 63 between Alston and Haltwhistle, a little moss-encrusted here and there but mostly in good nick, according to Stuart. Also in fine fettle was the imposing Lambley Viaduct, a few miles beyond Slaggyford, and just waiting for trains to pass over it once more. Built in 1852, it soared to a height of over 110ft and spanned a distance of 800yds. The viaduct was restored in 1996, and in 2013 it passed on from the now defunct North Pennine Heritage Trust into the hands of the South Tynedale Railway Preservation Society – a statuesquely symbolic statement of belief in its commitment to extend this line to Lambley and beyond. The society

Alston station in the British Rail days, 1965

Steam loco No. 10 Naklo *at Alston on the relaid narrow-gauge line, 1995*

had also secured another picturesque viaduct on the outskirts of Haltwhistle itself.

For today, however, the final halt was at Lintley. As we approached, the sun that had been shafting through the clouds here and there all morning suddenly lit up the hills, the fields and the sheep grazing in them as if to bathe the future in optimism.

Beyond a shelter painted in evocative maroon and cream was a sign to the Kirkstyle Inn offering real ale, river views and 'great food' (including Northumberland rather than Cumberland sausages, apparently). Not much more than two miles, the sign said. 'More like four,' Stuart had reckoned. Mmm … another time, maybe. It was a bit early in the day for a pint, even for Mick and me.

Across the line from the platform were the remains of one of many mines on which the local economy had once depended. Apart from coal, there was a lot of lead and zinc in these parts. I'll never forget going into a disused lead mine not too far from here. It had been considerably warmer in there than on the icy pavements and snow-capped hills outside. The Carrs mine up at Nenthead, just to the south of Alston, had closed in 1921, putting 400 miners out of work. A mixed blessing, you might say. Lead miners suffered not only from silicosis – a serious lung disease caused by repeatedly inhaling dust –but also from blood poisoning caused by a smelting process that gave off gases and particles. Quite a few lost eyes as well, through a drilling routine that involved sticking gunpowder in the hole and tapping it with an iron bar.

Today the town of Alston's population was less than 2,000, compared to nearly 7,000 in the 1840s when mining was at its peak. There was just one family-owned drift mine left.

'Anything else?' I asked the chairman of the parish council, Alan Green, when I rang him a couple of days later.

'There's still a stone quarry and a little foundry, plus somebody that makes candles, and a specialist in office equipment.'

Apart from that, the local economy seemed to be dependent on sheep farming and tourism. So it won't be a surprise to learn that the parish council was fully behind plans to extend the narrow-gauge railway. 'Eventually it could provide a real bonus for Alston by bringing in visitors, particularly at weekends and holiday times,' said Alan. 'But at the moment it doesn't really go anywhere.'

Well, not unless you fancy a hike through glorious countryside with the promise of Roman remains or a Northumberland sausage washed down with a decent pint while enjoying a river view.

On the return journey we shared a somewhat more sparse and Spartan carriage with two young lads, teenagers by the look of them, with expensive-looking cameras, who had been taking pictures of locomotives and carriages with the intensity of paparazzi outside a

Alston station signal box with snow plough, 1950s

hotel full of celebrities. 'We just love trains,' one of them told me before comparing shots with his mate all the way back.

Before hitting all-too-literally the high spots of Alston, there was time for a quick nose around the signal box. There was an old-fashioned black phone in there that didn't work, and an old-fashioned Eastern Railways clock that did. But then knowing the right time must be quite important when you're in here. You have to know what's coming the other way, and at how many minutes past the hour. And bearing in mind that the whole point of these narrow-gauge lines was to offer us glimpses into the past, signal boxes like this were not computerised. Instead it offered a long line of lengthy levers just waiting to be gripped and yanked. The man yanking them today was Martin Ashley. Or should I say Professor Ashley. Yes, this was the jolly gent in the yellow jacket who had waved us off on the 10.45. Emeritus professor, I should have said, as he had pretty well retired from Edge Hill University. Academics, like freelance journalists, rarely retire entirely.

'And your specialist subject?' I enquired, in the manner of John Humphrys on *Mastermind*.

'Male adolescent voices.'

You didn't have to be an academic to work out that Martin's own voice, far from adolescent as it was, didn't have an accent from around here. 'Kent?' I suggested.

'That's right,' he said, sounding quite impressed (or may be that was my imagination). 'My grandfather was the chief engineer on the old LMS line,' he added by way of explanation for his involvement with this railway. That often seemed to be the way with volunteers on narrow-gauge lines. A love of trains was inherited from those who once relied on railways to earn their living.

It was pleasantly warm in the signal box, even though there were only ashes in the open fireplace and the pile of kindling by the door appeared to have been undisturbed. 'It's sometimes easier just to switch on the electric radiator,' Martin admitted.

Warmth was in short supply half an hour later when we stood atop the sweeping, steep and cobbled main street in Alston after a tendon-tautening trek uphill.

Well worth the effort, mind you. The summit was breathtaking in more ways than one. From here you could see open moorland soaring above the slate roofs of ancient buildings before disappearing behind the spire of St Augustine's Church. In the foreground was the pointed roof of the Market Cross, first built in 1764, at the sharp bend halfway up the hill.

Like the rolling stock on the railway, the 'shopping offer' on the high street was an eclectic mix. Opposite the grand town hall was a hardware store that my dad would have loved. It sold everything from packets of screws to watering cans, spades, coal scuttles and much more. I wouldn't have been surprised to find a paraffin heater in there and a can of Esso Blue. Higher up the cobbles was a wholefood shop offering specialist mustards and cheeses as well as remedies and recipes. Nearby was a place where you could buy anything from a multi-coloured hippy jacket that would have been cool in 1967 to a pack of sensible thermal socks. Very warm at any time, I should imagine. Next door was a bookshop with a diverse selection of titles, including *Trout Fishing with Tom Saville*, *The Reflexology Handbook* and an architectural guidebook to Venice.

Further up still was an old clock shop that also offered clothing alterations, and an equestrian specialist in bridles and saddles. Yes, there was a butcher's a chemist and a post office as well. Plus a rather impressive late-Victorian building that once housed the Carlisle and Cumberland Bank. It looked like a reminder of the days when bankers were pin-striped pillars of probity. Long closed, alas, although a cash machine flashed forlornly on that exterior of faded opulence as if to say, 'We do still offer money, you know.'

By now it was past one o'clock, and all this exercise was evidently giving us an appetite. We repaired to the Angel Inn for soup, ham sandwiches and a splendid pint of Black Sheep bitter from down south in Yorkshire. These days I rarely drink at lunchtime, but what the hell.

It turned out to be a satisfying way to round off an exhilarating visit. Once again I'd witnessed the quiet, understated determination and dedication of volunteers who'd helped to reopen a long-closed railway against the odds. Once again I'd been shown an extraordinary collection of rolling stock from widely diverse sources. Once again I'd made a little journey into the past, and once again I'd driven – or at least *been* driven – through soaring hills of rugged beauty in another remote and under-populated part of a beautiful small island that we city-dwellers tend to think of as overcrowded.

Difficult to believe that within two days I would be on the Norfolk Broads, waiting to catch another little train.

13

A BANKER AND A BEAR ON THE BROADS

THE BURE VALLEY RAILWAY

Yes, I remember Worstead. Not exactly Adlestrop, but a lovely rustic part of England all the same. All the birds of Norfolk and Suffolk were out there somewhere on those flattish fields around the station. Including bitterns, presumably. Well, this was and still is the 'Bittern Line', running from Norwich to Sheringham. Now, as you may have gathered from previous chapters, I wouldn't know a bittern if it bit me – and, having just looked at a picture of one online, I'm damn glad one hasn't. What a beak!

I digress.

Worstead only came to mind because here I was on the Bittern Line again, for the first time in over 15 years. It must have been just after the turn of the century when I'd gone there to interview a man called Eric Sadler, a character who might have stepped straight out of the turn of the previous century. His job it was to push open the level crossing gates whenever a train approached, and then push them shut again once it had departed. That's what he was paid for, anyway. But Eric did more than that. Much more.

A former farm worker, he told me in his rich Norfolk drawl, 'If I'm bashing, knocking or scraping, I'm happy.' Digging, too, he could have added, having turned the garden he'd created around that little idyll of a station into a dazzling array of blooms. Every now and then he would clean out an oil drum and send it up the line to West Runton so that the local Women's Institute could make jam in it. They'd send him back a selection of blackcurrant, damson and raspberry. And if he was on a Sunday shift, he'd serve his family a full roast beef dinner, cooked in the station's Baby Belling and served at 1.05 prompt, as soon as he'd seen off the one o'clock train and checked on the Yorkshires.

Well, what you might call 'push-to' level crossings have long since gone the same way as signal boxes with old-fashioned levers. On mainline railways, anyway. But I'd still been looking forward to peering out of the window to see what remained of Eric's idyll – until, that is, it dawned on me that Worstead was one stop beyond Hoveton and Wroxham where I had to get off. Still, at least there was the prospect of another journey into the past.

There were no automatic gates on the Bure Valley Railway. In fact, no gates at all on the 9-mile journey

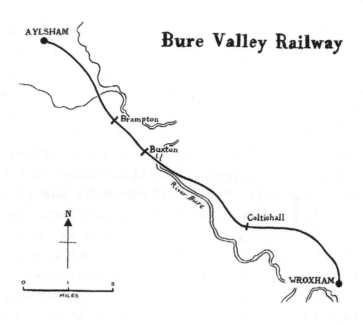

from Wroxham to Aylsham. Yes, it crossed a few roads here and there, but they tended to be narrow, mainly deserted country lanes on which you might expect to see a hay wain and nothing more. There were cars, of course, but I imagined they'd be few and far between. The engine stops, gives a warning hoot and sallies forth, except on those rare occasions when some traffic is passing by.

Like the Ravenglass and the Romney, Hythe and Dymchurch, the Bure Valley ran on a 15in gauge. Unlike them, however, it was family-owned. Andrew Barnes and his wife Susan Munday had taken a controlling interest in the railway in 2001. Andrew used to work in an investment bank in the City, and Susan was in accountancy, so it was perhaps not surprising that they had made the line financially viable for the first time.

My appointment with Andrew was in Aylsham at around 5.30, which meant that I could catch the last train of the day, the 16.40. That still left some time for a stroll around the town. After all, Wroxham is billed as the 'capital of the Broads'. Or should that be Wroxham and Hoveton? The two very small towns are connected by a broad bridge over an impressive expanse of water. Both are also dubbed as 'Roys Town', because what we must now learn to call the shopping offer is dominated by a family-owned company dubbed 'The World's Largest Village Store'. On the short walk from the station was 'Roys long-stay coach and car park'. A few hundred yards further on were Roys Food Hall, Roys Toys, Roys Children's World and Roys Pharmacy. But the first thing I saw on strolling into the food hall was a branch of McDonald's. The world's largest village store, it seemed, hosted the world's largest 'restaurant' and takeaway.

Not far away I glanced up and saw – good grief – Roys 'Indian Cuisine'. But on closer inspection it turned out to be a curry house called the Royal. All I wanted was a cuppa, and I found the ideal spot on the other side of that broad bridge. It was comparatively warm for the time of year, so I sat outside as the sun glinted on the wide and placid waters of the River

Aylsham station staff line-up, 1912

Aylsham station c.1920s/30s

Bure and owners busied themselves around boats so long and sleek they looked as though they might be turbocharged.

A waitress who looked about 12 brought me a pot of tea and a substantial slice of delicious lemon cake. With a pastry fork, if you please. 'There's posh,' as they say in Wrexham rather than Wroxham. Another country. Another world. Same small island. Had it been only two days ago that I'd been on the South Tynedale line in the ear-popping hills of Cumbria and Northumberland? Same country, very different landscape – or waterscape in this case. Down river from here, the Broads begged to be explored. And you didn't need to own a boat of your own to do it. 'You can have an hour and a half on here and a trip on the train for 20 quid all in,' I was told by someone in charge of one of the tall pleasure craft casting its reflection on the mirrored surface of the Bure. By 'the train' he meant the narrow-gauge one I was meant to be catching.

It was time to go back to the mainline station and walk slightly beyond to the Wroxham end of the Bure Valley line, where wildly excited children were awaiting the 16.40, otherwise known as the 'Spooky Express'. It was still half-term, and Halloween was just a few days away. One of the parents, I noticed, was lighting a crafty roll-up while the kids gazed open-mouthed at the jagged-toothed pumpkin with nose and piercing eyes that had been affixed to the front of the gleaming steam engine. Whether they were really spooked or simply baffled by seeing a pumpkin fronting a steam engine was difficult to tell. I was about to ask them when their mum stubbed out her nub-end and ushered them aboard a rapidly filling carriage.

The 'Spooky Express' would travel at a maximum of 20 miles per hour, but these 15in-gauge trains have a low centre of gravity, which gives a real sensation of speed while still offering plenty of time to savour the surrounding countryside. Very different countryside from the South Tynedale line, but it wasn't as flat as Norfolk is sometimes assumed to be. It undulated at regular intervals and embankments, strewn with brown bracken and brambles, were surprisingly steep in parts. As one of the drivers would tell me on the return journey the following morning, this line put considerable strain on a train.

For now I didn't want to think about tomorrow. It was quite entrancing watching the sun beginning to set over the distant horizon to the left. Just occasionally you'd catch sight of a scene worthy of Constable. Yes, I know he came from over the border in Suffolk, but grazing horses, tree-fringed ponds, church spires and stone cottages are common to both counties.

So, too, are great swathes of arable land. To both sides of the train were fields full of vegetables, plains of ploughed soil or the stubbly remains of long-since-harvested wheat. Closer to the train was a footpath strewn with crunchy-looking brown leaves.

Occasionally you'd see a dog walker stop and wave to us and, in one case, a woman striding so fast that she could well have been taking part in some stringent exercise regime. Or maybe she just wanted to get home before darkness fell. The nearer we came to Aylsham, the more lights were coming on – headlights passing occasionally on distant lanes and bulbs lighting up the small number of buildings adjoining the railway. Autumn was certainly deepening, and the nights were drawing in. Those cottages were few and far between, and what comparatively modern housing there was tended to be clustered around the four or five halts.

There was a passing loop at Hautbois, offering a chance to take a closer look at Hautbois Hall, built in 1553 as a Tudor manor house with architectural flamboyance galore, including fancy brickwork, mullioned windows and chimneys from which Lutyens might have found inspiration. These days the hall was a wedding venue. As one who has shelled out more than enough on weddings, I shudder to think how much a photographic backdrop like Hautbois would cost.

This being the Spooky Express, seasonal Halloween pictures had been pinned to trees or fences or the backs of farm buildings all the way down the line. Children had sheets on which they could tick off sightings of either friendly-looking ghosts or pumpkins with very slightly menacing faces. 'We've got 25 between us!'

announced Amy Peplow as we passed through a lengthy
tunnel under the Aylsham by-pass. By 'we' she meant
herself and her nine-year-old twin Aaron. I felt
privileged to be sharing a carriage with this friendly
family from Sudbury in Suffolk. Apart from Aaron,
Amy and an enormous toy duck she had lugged with
her, there were Mum and Dad, Charmaine and Tony,
13-year-old Katie who had cerebral palsy, and her
delightful carers Carol and Helen. Katie used a
wheelchair, and it was heartening to see a narrow-
gauge line ensuring that a disabled person was not
treated like a piece of luggage and confined to the
equivalent of the guards van. 'All the carriages we've
built here are wheelchair-accessible,' Andrew Barnes
assured me when I met him in the cafe at Aylsham
Station. Quite right, too.

He was casually dressed, and the enthusiasm with
which he later showed me an impressively varied
rolling stock in the engine shed was more than just a
public relations exercise. Nostalgia for steam, however,
was neither softening nor befuddling the formidable
business brain all too evidently lurking behind that
broad forehead.

But Andrew, how come a City investment banker
came to be managing director of a narrow-gauge
railway in deepest rural Norfolk?

'My father worked for the railways as a civil engineer
from 1960 until 1998,' he said. 'And I first saw this line

and took photos of it back in the late seventies or early eighties, when it was still a main line carrying freight.'

Not for much longer, as it turned out. The main line had closed for good in 1982, 30 years after it had stopped carrying passengers. The freight included coal being transported from Norfolk Thorpe Station to Norwich City Station via Aylsham – an extraordinarily long journey to get the black stuff from one side of the city to the other. Not a very profitable detour, I should imagine.

And the lack of profit had continued after the line had been converted to narrow-gauge and reopened in 1990 under private ownership. To cut a long story short, when Andrew had become involved as a volunteer in 1997 it was £980,000 in debt. 'It had been run by a consortium that couldn't agree on much,' he confided. 'Finally I was approached by each of the two divided sides, and agreed to take over their interests. But I was still living in Bedfordshire and working in London. We didn't move to Norfolk until 2009. That's when Susan became business manager and marketing director. But I continued commuting to London every day, and didn't resign from my banking job and become managing director here until 2014.'

'Does Susan like railways?'

'Yes. But that wasn't the only factor. It was the challenge of taking on a business and making it financially viable. Believe it or not, this railway used to be closed at half-term! Yet yesterday was our busiest day of the year so far. We're now open 252 days a year, and we have over 120,000 visitors annually.'

'Doesn't it get a bit nippy out there in the winter months?'

'All our carriages have electric heating. What's more, the cafe and the shop stay open every day, apart from Christmas Day and Boxing Day. We've also built up a model railway business by mail order. And apart from the combined train-and-boat ticket, societies such as the Women's Institute or the University of the Third Age can charter a train for a day with lunch at the cafe thrown in. Three years ago we went debt-free, and we've stayed that way. If we don't have the money, we don't spend it, and we re-invest. We wash our own face...'

Eh? A term used in the City presumably. What did that mean?

'We get no external grants.'

The railway did, though, have a very active group of 'Friends', some 450-strong, and they made a significant financial contribution. 'Last year we handed over a cheque for £40,000,' their chairman Ken Girven told me. They ran two second-hand bookshops at either end of the line, with all the books donated. At the larger of the two, on the station platform at Wroxham, the shelves had been better stocked than many a local library – everything from the almost-complete works of Dickens to romantic fiction, gardening and cookery books, and a children's section featuring Rupert Bear and the *Jack and Jill Annual* from 1976.

Table 57   NORWICH (Thorpe), WROXHAM, AYLSHAM (South),
COUNTY SCHOOL, and DEREHAM

	Week Days only							Week Days only						
Miles	p.m	a.m.	a.m.	p.m	p.m	p.m			a.m.	a.m.	a.m.	a.m.	a.m.	p.m
											S	S	E	
	3 London (L. St.) dep							54 London (L'pool St) dep			5 50		5 50	8 20
—	Norwich (Thorpe) .. dep							Dereham .... dep					12 0	
1¼	Whitlingham A							North Elmham ...... arr						
6	Salhouse							County School ... { arr } { dep }						
8¼	Wroxham .... { arr } { dep }							Foulsham						
11½	Coltishall							Reepham (Norfolk)						
14¼	Buxton Lamas							Cawston						
17½	Aylsham (South)							Aylsham (South)						
22	Cawston							Buxton Lamas						
24	Reepham (Norfolk) ..							Coltishall						
28½	Foulsham							Wroxham .... { arr } { dep }						
32½	County School ... { arr } { dep }							Salhouse						
34	North Elmham							Whitlingham A						
38¼	Dereham .... arr							Norwich (Thorpe) .. arr						
163½	54 London (L.St.).. arr							3 London (L'pool St) arr						

A Station for Thorpe St. Andrew
a a.m.
B Runs 15th July to 9th September inclusive
C 3 minutes later on Saturdays
E Except Saturdays

F The East Anglian.   Limited accommodation
L Via Norwich (Thorpe) Dep. 1 0 p.m. on Wednesdays and 1 3 p.m. on Saturdays

N Arr. 5 6 p.m. until 24th June
P Dep. 10 25 a.m. on Saturdays
p p.m.
S or S Saturdays only
Z Dep. 11 25 p.m. on Sundays

For **OTHER TRAINS** between Norwich and Whitlingham, Tables 55 and 58—Norwich and Wroxham, Table 55—Norwich and County School, Table 54—County School and Dereham; Table 54.

A 1950 timetable for the British Railways train service through Aylsham and Wroxham

British Railways Class E4 steam locomotive 62797 at Aylsham station, 1952

There was a record section as well, with vinyl much in evidence. The first album I'd picked up featured Frankie Vaughan. Then there was a Cliff Richard album that went back to his days with the Shadows. The first single I spotted was by Chas & Dave. What you might call 'heritage music' evidently has a market among the narrow-gauge travellers of Norfolk.

Back on Aylsham Station, it was pitch-dark when Andrew and I emerged from the cafe and headed for the shed, or rather the workshop where volunteers were still cleaning and polishing, restoring or overhauling an impressive array of steam engines, with a couple of diesels thrown in. 'What I like about narrow-gauge trains,' Andrew was saying, 'is that they have character and individuality. No two are the same.'

We'd been joined by the railway's general manager, David Lowe, a former teacher and volunteer who was now one of 17 paid staff. He pointed out an immaculately maintained stalwart of the line with a colourful history. 'It was paid for by a wealthy gent to work on a line in Antigua. But he died before they finished building it. So they somewhat hastily put it together, installed a diesel engine, and sold it to Dudley Zoo in 1964. It's been to multiple locations since, including Blenheim Palace. In 1991 it came here, and we restored it as a proper steam engine and renamed it the *Wroxham Broad*. It's the smallest in the fleet, but it would still walk away with the carriages on that steep gradient at

Ravenglass. The drivers love it, because there are times when you can really open it out…'

By now it was time to bid farewell to the *Wroxham Broad*, as well as Andrew and David, and go off in search of the Black Boys. No, not another engine but rather the pub where I'd booked a room for the night. Quite a historic pub, as it turned out, overlooking the market place in Aylsham. According to a plaque on the pub frontage, Admiral Lord Nelson had attended a ball at the assembly rooms here in 1792. Hope he managed to get something to eat before hitting the dance floor. Having perused a mouthwatering menu while savouring a pint of Norfolk's own Woodford Wherry, I discovered that every table was taken. Popular pub, the Black Boys. There might be a table free later, I was told. And maybe not, presumably.

At least there were plenty of seats in the Gate of India restaurant a few doors away. Sitting in splendid isolation, I was able to see off a delicious king prawn biryani while chatting to the manager about cricket. No, he wasn't too keen on Twenty-20 either. As for the big money swirling around the Indian Premier League, I realised that it was a mistake to get him started on that. We were both die-hard aficionados of longer forms of the game, it transpired, as we shook hands warmly and parted company.

Unfortunately, the next English home Test series seemed a long way away the following morning as Aylsham basked in a low, autumnal sun. A hundred yards or so from the Black Boys was the parish church of St Michael and All Angels, a large cruciform-shaped building in handsome stone with a curious small spire jutting over the turrets of the tower. It was early in the day and Biddy's Tea Room at the gateway to the church was still closed. But for those who like that kind of thing, Biddy's did brew an extraordinary selection of teas: almond, violet, black vanilla and many more. Nearby was an exotic chocolate shop and a florist called Lavender Blue, the exterior of which was painted in a startling shade of pink with mauve window frames.

Back at the station, David was about to climb into a bear suit. All part of the general manager's job at school-holiday time, apparently. Well, at least he didn't have to dress up as a pumpkin. 'It can get incredibly hot in there,' he confided shortly before reappearing on the platform, ursine from head to toe, and waving to the children on the 10 o'clock train to Wroxham. At one point, he opened the carriage door to shake my hand, much to the surprise of three-year-old Cody, who was on a day trip to the Broads with his aunt, Suzanne Evans.

'What's that bear come in here for?' Cody wanted to know. He stuck his head out of the window. 'I think he's coming back,' he proclaimed. 'Hope so!'

Well before we'd reached Wroxham, Cody had discovered a new pastime. Shouting in my ear at regular intervals was far more fun than looking out of the window at 'animals' (horses for the most part) and fishermen setting up their pitch for the day on the banks of the Bure. As a grandfather of seven, I know how to feign surprise in these circumstances. But the more I pretended to be shocked, the more Cody bawled '*Boo!*' with ever-increasing volume and no little delight, despite Suzanne's valiant attempts to restrain him.

By the time we reached the end of the line, I was partially deaf in one ear. At least I could just about hear what our driver, Roger Danes, was saying in answer to my question about the gradients (or lack of them) in Norfolk. 'Yes, it's comparatively flat compared to, say, Ravenglass, which I've also driven on, but there you go up one way and down the other. Here it's constantly undulating. In fact, there are only two really flat parts, and' – he gestured at the platform – 'you're standing on one of them. It means that the engine is either pulling hard or shutting off. You can't relax. As soon as we set off, he's shovelling coal.'

'He' being the fireman, in case you hadn't guessed. Matt Howard was 21 and had started volunteering here when he was 15. 'I'm hoping to pass out as a driver soon,' he said. And your day job, Matt? 'I'm a chef at a school in Essex.' There was a pause while I glanced at his blackened fingers. 'Don't worry,' he grinned. 'I do give my hands a good scrub.'

Roger was considerably older than 21, but still working as a BBC outside-broadcast engineer. 'It's an irregular working pattern, which means that I can slot in a day up here every now and then. I live in London.'

London? That reminded me. I needed to be on the 11.25 to Norwich to catch my connection south. As I stood on the mainline platform, I could see the steam rising from the return train to Aylsham.

Yes, I'd remember Wroxham and Aylsham as well as Worstead just up the line from here. I'd remember them when we finally pulled into Liverpool Street with its corporate shops and food stalls. The more our stations, shopping centres and high streets house the same chain stores, takeaways, coffee bars and street furniture, the more tempting it is to think that the UK is becoming more uniform. But trundling around its more remote parts had proved to be a way of reminding myself that, in other respects, this small island was anything *but* uniform. It remained a place of infinite variety, and its contrasts, from Devil's Bridge to Dungeness, Wroxham to Ravenglass, were best savoured through the window of a sedately paced narrow-gauge railway.

14

THE DREAM THAT NEVER QUITE DIED

THE SOUTHWOLD RAILWAY

Even in the fading light of a late November afternoon, there was something rather charming about Southwold Harbour. The lights were already on in the Harbour Inn, as well as in the stall selling some of the fresh fish landed by those boats bobbing around in their moorings. No pleasure craft evident today. They would be back in the summer, presumably, including a yacht which apparently would make *Britannia* look a little on the small side.

But John Ridgway and I were not here to look at boats or to buy fish. We were peering at a piece of metal. And there it was, protruding from a patch of mud that looked about as inviting as quicksand. That short stretch of jutting rust was all that remained of the original track of the Southwold Railway in the position that it was laid.

The railway opened in 1879, and ran on a 3ft gauge between Halesworth and Southwold, a distance of just under 9 miles. 'That bit of rail was part of an extension to the harbour, which they started in 1912 when the fishing industry was at its peak,' said John, a prominent member of the Trust trying to revive Suffolk's railway heritage. 'They finished it just in time for the First World War when fishing collapsed.'

Thankfully the collapse wasn't permanent. Fish was part of the freight carried by the railway for most of the 1920s, along with coal, farm produce, newspapers and Adnams Ale. Then, as now, you could have any beer you liked in the Southwold area as long as it was brewed by Adnams.

And the fish?

Well, that was transferred to the main line at Halesworth, and would still be bright-eyed when slapped on to a slab in Billingsgate Market. Long before the advent of the M11, it seems, links between London and Southwold were essential to the town's prosperity. These days, of course, a number of City bankers and other metropolitan 'moneybags' own second homes in that delightful seaside town. Not to mention beach huts at a price that would buy a row of terraced houses in Rotherham or Rochdale. Back in the late 19th and early 20th centuries, it was less prosperous Londoners who were prominent among the holidaymakers who flocked here in the summer months. They'd board the

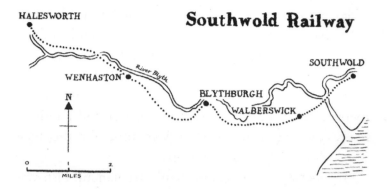

main line at Liverpool Street, and change to the narrow-gauge at Halesworth.

Among them was one Wynn Riddell, whose story was recorded over 20 years ago for a book called *The Southwold Railway Children*. Wynn's mother had married a Londoner, but she came originally from one of the oldest longshore fishing families in the town. Every June, she would take Wynn back home for a family reunion and a holiday. Until 1929 that is, when stiff competition from a local bus service brought about the railway's closure, much to Wynn's chagrin. 'I was heartbroken,' she revealed. 'It was the end of an era. I wasn't here, because I was at school in London and I couldn't pop down for the end of it. It was the end of the old Southwold really...'

Earlier in the same interview, she had given a fond description of what it was like to travel on that scenic line:

'The railway engine had a really tall funnel at the front, and the seats were facing one another like the old trams used to be, with stair carpet along the seats, so if you were wriggling with excitement you had very sore legs by the time you got to Southwold.'

As for that tall-funnelled engine, it 'gasped a little' on a steep stretch after stopping at Wenhaston,

'and we all prayed it got to the top. Then from Wenhaston to Blythburgh and all along the banks, as it was June, there were pink valerian flowers which a little London girl thought were really beautiful growing alongside the track. Then, from Blythburgh we'd go through the herony which was really lovely. There were pine trees on either side of the track… Eventually we arrived in Walberswick. The station there was right on the other side of the heath, so if any passengers had luggage they had quite a long walk… Then, over the old bridge… through the cutting and [we] arrived eventually at Southwold Station which, in June, had big flowerbeds full of cornflowers…'

That station is now a car park behind the police station. And all that's left of the terminus at the Halesworth end are the concrete foundations of the engine shed. The line in between the two towns was finally torn up in 1941 and the metal donated to the war effort. So was the rolling stock, which had lain dormant

Railway station, Southwold, 1929

Southwold Railway, early 1900s

for 12 years. Nothing had moved since the last train at 5.23 on 11 April 1929. An Act of Parliament was required to dissolve the statutory company that owned the railway, and the cost was prohibitive – in peacetime at least. As for the bridge over the River Blythe, that was blown up to impress the wartime 'top brass' in a scene worthy of *Dad's Army*. It has since been replaced by a footbridge.

There's very little of the original railway left. Apart, that is, from that little stretch of track in the mud by the harbour, and the former coal shed at Blythburgh that's still standing. Just about. 'This must be the only thing holding it up,' said John Ridgway (remember him?), my guide for the afternoon, as we groped our way through the foliage of some sturdy bush that had completely enveloped the original structure. There were holes in the roof and holes in the side where bits of corrugated iron dangled down. Ivy wound its way around what remained of the door. And the floor? That was covered with bags of dumped rubbish, an old vacuum cleaner, a bottle of pop and a couple of tyres. Not a lump of coal to be seen. As for the trackbed, that ran alongside the shed here on a patch of wasteland just off the A12.

We would see a lot more of that bed once we reached Wenhaston, where the Southwold Railway Trust had acquired 33 acres of land, before selling 30 of them to a local farmer. The remaining three acres were part of the Trust's long-term ambition to revive the line. If and when they get planning permission, that is. That's a big 'if'. The owner of a substantial adjacent property with a lengthy garden is just one of the objectors. 'In fact, the track once ran through that garden, before curving gently to the left and along here,' John pointed out as we walked the quarter of a mile or so that the volunteers had cleared. To the left was a drainage ditch and open fields, to the right some arable farmland. 'Fifteen of us did the clearance work over a period of four months.'

'Any youngsters among you?'

'Not any more,' he replied drily. 'There were a lot of brambles along here, as well as dead elms, elders and oaks. Luckily most of us are retired with time to spare.'

It wasn't just a matter of hacking through the undergrowth and chopping back overhead branches. Here were the stunted trunks of three oak trees that had been chopped down.

'We consulted local environmentalists first and they said that five of them were too close together and none of them are thriving. Remember,' John went on, 'that they've grown since the line was torn up.' He then unveiled a crop of saplings: 'For every tree we've taken down, we're planting another ten.'

Brand new fencing had been installed all the way along the trackbed. And what was this if it wasn't a new stretch of track? New sleepers, anyway. New rails too, for the most part. Little scraps of the original line had apparently been recovered from here and there.

For the time being, however, this short stretch remained a statement of intent. Nothing more. Although planning permission to run trains through here was originally recommended by Suffolk Coastal District Council officers, councillors refused the application. The Trust took its application to an appeal, but the planning inspectors dismissed it.

At least the Trust's other statement of intent seemed more likely to go ahead. Indeed, by the time you read this, work should be well underway on building a new station at Southwold, not far from the original, on the site of a decontaminated former gas works. There wasn't much to see this afternoon as John and I peered through the fence, other than some buddleia bushes and a few substantial rubbish bins. There was also an adjacent allotment that was there in the railway's day, and a row of houses that wasn't. The original trackbed ran across what were now their lawns and flowerbeds. John grinned broadly. 'One resident has already suggested that if we want some ballast, all we have to do is dig over her garden.' Which suggests that there is support as well as opposition to plans to revive the railway.

Earlier that afternoon we'd met at the offices of another prominent trustee – another John. John Bennett was an architect: I asked him where the main opposition was coming from.

Incomers, was the gist of his reply. 'The locals are in favour for the most part. There's something about the steam and mechanics of these old locomotives that the public love. And unlike modern mainline trains, there are no electric cables suspended above the track. Yet every time we make a planning application it's mainly the second-home owners who raise a hue and cry. Although they'd never say it outright, they don't like tourists. And, yes, admittedly the traffic here can be murder in the summer months. But under our plans, visitors would be able to park and ride. There'd be a car park just off the A12, and they could get on the train and come into the centre of town. In the early 1900s that was part of the holiday.'

John B, as we'll call him to distinguish him from John R, told me that he liked the 'idiosyncratic' character of narrow-gauge railways. Well, there was certainly something idiosyncratic about his shop-front reception here on the High Street. Apart from the leather-bound tomes around the walls, there was a telescope on the desk, a brace of pistols under a clock, and in the window was a typewriter so ancient that it pre-dated the monstrous clatterers I used to pound away on in the heady days of multi-edition newspapers.

The computer in the corner looked somewhat incongruous in such a setting, but John B would sit down at it every now and then to print off various plans he had drawn up for the old gasworks site. Apart from a 'multi-purpose' station building, there would be a museum and a workshop to house the Trust's growing collection of 3ft-gauge rolling stock. Most of the one-acre site would be 'sculpted into a mini-nature reserve', and visitors would be transported around it on a 7½-inch miniature railway.

'We've had to meet 18 planning conditions,' the architect confided. 'The idea is to set up a little tourist attraction, and we'll see where it goes from there.' Well, certainly you need a station building for planners to begin to take you seriously, as the South Tynedale had shown.

John B could be described as a bit of an incomer himself. He had moved to the east coast from London's Camden Town some 25 years earlier. And he had certainly left his mark on Southwold town, with some highly distinctive buildings, including the Electric Picture Palace just down the road from his office – a stunning re-creation of an early cinema, complete with a Wurlitzer organ that rises through the floor at some stage of the proceedings. So perhaps his plans to revive the railway should not be underestimated, despite the opposition.

'I first floated the idea back in 1994, and advertised for potential members of what then would have been a society,' he recalled. 'Then I went off to America for a year. When I came back, there were about half a dozen people expressing an interest.'

From that has grown a Trust with over 400 members, including some in Canada, New Zealand and France.

Luckily, one of the original half-dozen lived a little closer. David Lee's house was next door to John B's office. David's recollections of the original railway were not as vivid as Wynn's, perhaps because he was a spring chicken of 94. 'One of my earliest memories was of sitting on my mother's knee and looking out at the rain hammering down on Halesworth Station,' he told me when we called in to see him. 'I must have been about two, and we must have been in coach number two, because it was the only one with an open balcony at the back,' he went on with the certainty of an unashamed railway buff. He would have been seven when the Southwold line came to an end exactly 50 years after it had opened. Any memories of that day?

'No, we were at our other house in St John's Wood.' (Ah, yes, the London connection again.) 'I do remember coming back here with my mother soon after it closed, and she was very concerned about getting all our cases on to the bus.'

As Marie Lloyd never quite sang,

'Oh, Mr Porter,
What's happened to our train?
I wanted to go to Southwold now,
and a bus won't take the strain.'

Who knows whether, a century on from its closure, that train will be running again all the way from Halesworth to Southwold? All I do know is that here, as in other far-flung beauty spots within these shores, a new breed of narrow-gauge pioneers has the know-how and the determination to make it happen, whatever the obstacles and whatever the opposition.

15

THE LAST GREAT RAILWAY ADVENTURE

THE LYNTON AND BARNSTAPLE RAILWAY

It was Saturday morning and I'd set the alarm early. Not that it made much difference. The motorways were still congested, the road works interminable, the long and winding A-class roads at the Devon end of the M5 likewise. Some four and a half hours after I'd set off, the gateway to Woody Bay Station suddenly appeared beyond the windscreen wipers. By then I was beginning to ask myself why I had driven so far in order to travel about a mile on a narrow-gauge railway. That's as far as the Lynton and Barnstaple goes. For the time being, at least.

But if you think my journey sounded a little excessive, consider this revelation from Dave Tooke, who was running the railway's ticket office and shop:

'We have members in Australia who make a pilgrimage here once a year.'

'Get away!'

'I kid you not. Admittedly only two come *every* year,' he went on. 'Several others come every *other* year. And we had an Australian gentleman who came in a couple of weeks ago who wasn't even a member. He said: "I've been reading your website for years and promising myself a trip here."'

'So he traversed the globe in order to go one mile up the line?'

'Yes, as part of a visit to the UK.'

Such trivia as London, the Cotswolds and Shakespeare's birthplace could wait their turn, it seemed. The Lynton and Barnstaple had been his first priority, such is the attraction of that fabled name among railway lovers around the world. And not just in Australia, according to Dave, but in the United States, Canada, and New Zealand as well. Just imagine what a draw it could become if and when the planned extension came about...

Never mind that 'if'; let's just say 'when'. Within an hour of arriving at Woody Bay and being shown glimpses of the trackbed beyond Killington Lane Halt, where the line currently terminated, I began to sense a quiet but resolute determination to get the job done, come what may. The Trust behind the railway had already spent four years on proposals to extend the line by four miles south from Killington to Blackmoor Gate, at a cost of nearly £400,000. That's the sort of money you have to shell out these days on the necessary studies and surveys if you're serious about getting planning permission.

North Devon Council had already given its approval for that part of the line within its jurisdiction. The Exmoor National Park Authority had yet to sit down to consider a proposal that would provide visitors with rail as an alternative to road access to the Park's many beauty spots. Assuming it does eventually give permission, the stage after that would be the five miles north from Woody Bay to Lynton. By then what is being billed as 'The Last Great Railway Adventure' would have gathered an unstoppable momentum. One day, the full 19 miles of track would reunite the two

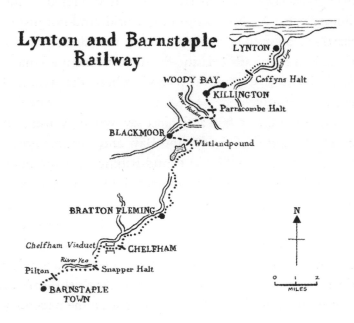

towns that the Lynton and Barnstaple linked until the Southern Railway closed it down in 1935. Died young, you might say. It was only 37 years old. 'I'm 59,' Dave confided, 'and I'm not sure that the full extension will happen in my lifetime.'

When you're approaching three-score it's easier to look back rather than forwards, and Dave certainly seemed to know plenty about the railway's history, from its recent past to its foundation. Between selling tickets for the 2.15 to well-muffled folk, he was able to give me what you might call a few lines on the Lynton. I was keen to know a bit more about Sir George Newnes, the London publisher who had put up the money for the railway back in the 1890s. He was founder of *Tit-Bits*, apparently, which women in particular seemed to find riveting when I was a kid. In 1891 he also brought out the *Strand* magazine, including as it did the first stories by one Arthur Conan Doyle about a detective called Sherlock Holmes. No wonder Sir George made a few bob.

'He bought a holiday home in Lynton and spent quite a bit of his personal fortune on various schemes to improve the lot of local people,' said Dave. 'Paid for the Town Hall as well as having a cliff railway built to link Lynton and Lynmouth.'

And that was just for starters. Generous George put up most of the money to link Lynton and Barnstaple by a narrow-gauge track of 1ft 11½in. It was finally open for business in 1898. Not that it ever made any money…

'The original station was in the wrong place,' Dave went on. 'The line was built to give the people of Lynton and Lynmouth access to the market town of Barnstaple, but they had to lug heavy bags and sometimes drag children right to the top of the hill.' As I would discover later, the streets of Lynton are as steep as Alston's – enough in parts to put a severe strain on taut tendons and set the heart pounding. To get up the highest of those highways could well require grappling hooks. The Trust planning to rebuild the line does not intend to make the same mistake. Meticulous as members have been in trying to recreate the railway exactly as it was, it seems likely that the end of the line at Lynton will be closer to the middle of town.

Having had his own large holiday home built here in North Devon, the last thing Sir George wanted was to encourage other holidaymakers and day-trippers. Perhaps he had heard stories of Welsh invaders coming over the Bristol Channel to escape from teetotal Sundays and slake prodigious thirsts, earned in hot and dusty mines for the most part, before scandalising the resorts of Ilfracombe and Minehead. The prospect of the English working class lurching into Lynton for their own bibulous day-trips was unthinkable. 'That's one of the reasons why this line was narrow-gauge,' Dave explained. 'That way there couldn't be through trains from Bristol, for instance. The day-trippers would carry on to Ilfracombe by standard gauge on the main line.'

At this point the guard popped into the ticket office and adjoining cafe to cry out, 'Anyone else for the 2.15?' Through the open door I could see the distinctive carriages, chocolate brown and cream, with gold lettering stamping them as 'Third'. Not that they looked third-class. Anything but. It's quite understandable that the Ffestiniog used them as models for its own restoration of passenger stock some 70 years after the L & B opened for business. 'Unlike the Welsh lines, this one was built first and foremost for passengers rather than freight,' Dave went on. 'The ones you can see today have been recreated from the originals. There were 17 originally, and they were cut up and sold off, mainly as garden furniture.' By that time the line was part of the Southern Railway – indeed, had been since 1922. 'Bits have been found here and there and held together with new materials to recreate the carriages as they were. We have a team of experts, all members, in Essex, where they have the space and the facilities to do that kind of thing. We only have a smallish engine shed here, where they can't do much apart from basic servicing.'

The Essex members were working on engines as well. The originals all had monosyllabic names, after Devon rivers. There was a *Yeo*, an *Exe* and a *Taw*. Also *Lyn*, built by the Baldwin Locomotive Works of Philadelphia. A *Lew*, too, sold at auction in 1935, shipped off to Brazil and never heard of again. At least a new *Lyn*, if not a new *Lew*, should be back on track next year, while a wealthy enthusiast has also, it seems, built himself a full-size replica L & B loco called *Lyd*, which currently resides on the Ffestiniog but makes regular visits to Devon.

So what was pulling those handsome carriages today?

Step, or rather roll, forward *Isaac*. He came from a platinum mine, and was one of two incomers from South Africa. 'We've also got a First World War loco, built by Kerr Stuart. That one's *Axe*,' Dave was telling me when we were joined by Tony Nicholson, one of the trustees of the Lynton and Barnstaple, a registered charity with over 2,500 members. A former history teacher, Tony had a splendid shock of wild, white hair that gave the impression that he had been in a high wind. That may well be because he had. The weather outside, at nigh-on a thousand feet above sea level, hadn't improved much, but Tony had promised to show me some of the trackbed on the proposed extension to Blackmoor Gate. It was time to face the elements again.

The mile-long train ride could wait. So could a closer look at Woody Bay Station, the acquisition of which in 1995 provided a further spur to turn the project from a distant dream into an achievable reality. The Lynton and Barnstaple Railway Association, which had been around since 1979, had finally acquired a headquarters and would soon turn itself into a trust.

'The next stage should take a couple of years fundraising, and a couple of years to build,' Tony was saying as we splashed across the puddles in the muddy car park. 'Volunteers will help with clearing the line, but I suspect we'll have to pay contractors to do the track-laying.'

After a mile or so he pulled off the road, and a hare went... well, haring across in front of us. The trains will go considerably slower as they come down the 1-in-50 gradient from Woody Bay. To get a better view, we climbed up a small tip of discarded tarmac and peered over a hedge as the valley unfolded beneath us. In the far distance the sun was shining on South Wales – 'I don't know what they've done to deserve that,' muttered Tony – and thin clouds were brushing the tops of hills like puffs of smoke. There was real smoke in the sublimely beautiful valley below, as the 14.30 (or was it the 15.15?) set off on its short journey back from Killington Lane.

Tony was pointing in the other direction: 'The line will do a huge loop, and go through a horseshoe shape, following the contours of the land and by-passing the really steep hills.'

The main street in Parracombe, the next village along, had a gradient of 1 in 4. 'Hopefully we won't meet the bus coming the other way, in which case I'm going to have to back up,' my chauffeur remarked drily as we passed one of two churches and a village store that was closed. What else would you expect on a Saturday afternoon?

At the bottom of the mercifully bus-free hill lay the Fox and Goose, which could be reached on foot from the halt at Killington Lane. 'That's the pub where we have our Trust meetings to plot our next conspiracy. It was rebuilt in 1894, the original having been gutted by fire. Used to be a coaching inn. The landlord lost trade when the railway opened, yet he was still a supporter. I think the navvies spent a hell of a lot of time and money here.'

And the 'navvies' of today?

'Well, we have between 50 and a hundred active volunteers, including what's known as the Thursday gang. They do some of the physical work that I couldn't and wouldn't. The existing track needs renewing from time to time.' As for the remains of the track*bed,* they were still clearly visible here and there, perhaps because of the efforts of those active volunteers in hacking back the undergrowth. There were even very occasional glimpses of a few feet of the original track. Most of it was flogged off by the Southern, along with the rolling stock, back in the 1930s.

As I had already heard, the railway had many more members worldwide. 'Some of them have been very generous,' Tony confided. Just as well. 'The next stage is going to cost around 16 million,' he went on. 'Nearly two million of that has already been spent.' On engines and carriages, for a start. Not forgetting station buildings, including the one just up the road from here at what was once Parracombe Halt.

We climbed out of the car again and stood on the original railway bridge to take a closer look. The slate roof of the building in question was just visible above high hedges and tall bushes. When we went around for a closer look, it turned out to be quite a substantial private detached house, built in formidable-looking grey stone, with a spreading oak tree nearby and horses in the field beyond. It came as no surprise to discover that the house was called Fair View. What was surprising is that planning permission had ever been given to a somewhat unprepossessing 1980s bungalow nearby. 'That's going to have to go,' said Tony. And Fair View? 'We've already bought that. It cost us £400,000, but that included quite a bit of trackbed. We'll sell it again.'

'To somebody who doesn't mind trains?'

'Well, the railway was here first, and it's not exactly the West Coast main line. In fact, a narrow-gauge enthusiast may well pay over the odds for it.'

At this point we were joined by a lady with a stick and a Labrador that appeared to be sporting miniature wellington boots on its front paws. 'When I was a girl, we used walk this line from Blackmoor Gate to Parracombe,' she told us, 'and I never imagined that it would ever reopen. I just hope it's going to happen in my lifetime.'

In case you're wondering, the distance from here to Blackmoor Gate was around 2.5 miles. And, no, we didn't have time to walk it. Apart from anything else, I

The Lynton and Barnstaple Railway's American-styled Lyn *stops for water at Blackmoor Gate*

A Lynton and Barnstaple Railway train near Chelfham around 1910

had a train to catch later. So instead of strolling down the trackbed, we climbed back into Tony's car and very soon we were pulling in to what appeared to be a pub car park. Like the one at Woody Bay, it was rather muddy and 'puddly' today. The former trackbed passed across it at one time, because the Old Station House Inn was, believe it or not, once the old station house, albeit with a 1950s extension at the front.

'We'll have to move the track slightly from where it ran originally, and restore the station as it was,' said Tony. And would there be room for the inn? Indeed there would. To quote from the Lynton and Barnstaple's official guide, 'The inn will be remodelled in keeping with the Victorian original to incorporate a restaurant, pub and tea-room as well as the station'.

And that's not all. 'This will be our main headquarters, complete with engine sheds,' Tony told me. 'They'll be down in that valley, completely hidden from the road.' The same unobtrusive and inconspicuous quality was also attributable to the mile of newish track that exists at the moment. I checked it as we drove back to Woody Bay. All you could see from the A39 was a lengthy line of hedge-like trees and the hills on the far side of the valley. The countryside here didn't surge and swoop as dramatically as it had in North Wales, but neither did it just roll or gently undulate. The valley was steep and stunningly picturesque. Sheep were scattered hither and yon. They all started running uphill at one point. Not because they were spooked by that green monster that kept chugging to and fro, breathing fire and issuing puffs of smoke, but because the farmer's dog was rounding them up. It was getting on for the end of the day, and Tony had joined me on the last train to Killington Lane.

Before climbing aboard, we'd grabbed a quick cup of tea in the cafe that now occupied what was once the stationmaster's parlour at Woody Bay. (No time for one of those Devon cream teas, alas.) The station's exterior had been restored to look exactly as it would have been when it was built in so-called Swiss-chalet style at a time when the Victorian promoters of the L & B were marketing the area as 'the English Switzerland'. I sat on an extremely comfortable former first-class seat, marvelling at the twirly moustache of a volunteer in overalls who had apparently been cleaning out the firebox. 'No, I haven't won any awards for it,' he said, referring to the moustache rather than his abilities with a shovel.

Before climbing aboard that last train, there was just time to call in at what is known as the 'Heritage Gents'. Yes, even the WC had been lovingly restored. In some ways it reminded me of those dimly lit latrines you used to find outside pubs after edging your way across some pitch-dark and windswept courtyard. This one was considerably cleaner, mind you. Even had liquid soap and paper towels.

We travelled out to Killington Lane at a stately 12 to 15 miles an hour. Just time to savour more of that ravishing view, as well as the immaculately painted cream-and-brown carriage interior. Even so, those wooden slatted seats might become a little uncomfortable if – no, *when* – the full 19 miles of the line are re-instated. 'We might have to provide some cushions,' Tony conceded.

On this occasion we had to wait only for *Isaac* to be turned round before heading back to Woody Bay. No time to indulge in the many beautiful walks hereabouts, or indeed to visit the Fox and Goose. This 2-mile return journey had been a little appetiser for a great feast to come. 'As the railway grows, the process will speed up,' said Tony. 'It will no longer seem just a pipe dream.' It was easy to see what he meant.

As is so often the case in this small island, Sunday morning proved to be very different from Saturday afternoon. It was glorious late-autumnal weather, and the sun was spilling on golden roadside leaves as I drove down narrow lanes to Chelfham, about 16 miles from Woody Bay and only 3 miles or so from Barnstaple. Suddenly the Chelfham Viaduct appeared, soaring over the trees to a height of 70ft as though flexing its pillars of pale-ish stone and exposing them to the sunlight. Each of its eight arches was 42ft wide, and somewhere down there, below a span of 400ft, was the comparatively piddling River Yeo. Mercifully and remarkably, the viaduct was listed in 1965, halfway through a decade that saw the destruction of many a magnificent piece of architecture. It had been built between 1896 and 1897 in preparation for the L & B's opening the following year. Just over a century later, it was restored by the Railways Heritage Trust. It was and is the largest narrow-gauge railway structure in England, and one day it will, believe me, support trains en route into Barnstaple once more.

To get up to the level of the viaduct by car you had to drive up a narrow, winding lane to what was Chelfham Station. Make that *is* Chelfham Station. Restoration was well on the way when I called in that glorious Sunday morning. No, there won't be any trains passing through in the near future. But, like Woody Bay before it, this was to be a statement of belief that it will happen one day. It was just before 10am, and the volunteers were soaking up the sun in fold-down chairs – a brief break with mugs of tea and, in some cases, sandwiches from a sizeable plastic box. Soon they would set to work again on the process of making this place look as it might have done at the turn of the last century. Minus the trains, but plus a working ladies' toilet that was not available in those days. Gentlemen were provided with what is described on the railway's website as 'a modest urinal', while ladies 'would have to hold on until Bratton Fleming'.

After seeing off the last of his tea from a Golden Age of Steam mug, the unofficial foreman Nigel Thompson gave me a quick guided tour of the site. Nigel drove delivery vans for Tesco during the week and spent his weekends helping to revive memories of a more romantic form of transport. 'We want to show this whole site off to visitors and give them some idea of the scale of ambition involved in rebuilding this railway,' he explained, leading the way past one shed full of tools and another with second-hand books for sale – railway books on one side and everything from *The White Wine Guide* to the complete works of Shakespeare on the other.

Just as on the Bure Valley Railway, any money raised from book sales or donations helped to pay for such items as the newish-looking fence lining the re-creation of a path to one of the former station platforms. 'That cost us about six hundred quid,' Nigel confided as I took in the former Southern Railway posters lined up along it in exactly the position they were when closure came in the mid-thirties. One advertised the joys of Bexhill-on-Sea, another Guernsey, 'the sunshine island'.

Beyond this small stretch of fence, the former trackbed disappeared into a line of nearby trees. Overhanging branches as well as bushes, brambles and much more had to be hacked back by a party of between 30 and 40 volunteers. Anybody visiting the station in future can walk that trackbed for a mile or so, as it's all part of the surrounding land acquired by the Railway Trust when it paid £175,000 in 1999 to acquire a site that had sold for £490 in 1941.

At the other end of the site, closer to the viaduct, was a short line of track. 'We found it stored here, and we've re-laid it in exactly the place where a siding was,' Nigel assured me, before going on to show me the station building. The original was smaller than Woody Bay, because the stationmaster evidently lived elsewhere. Just a waiting room and ticket office, then. Door and window in exactly the same position, needless to say. Log stove, too. Sawn-off church pews now provided the seating. And the 'Ladies'? That could also be used by gents.

The volunteers were still in the process of demolishing a characteristically lacklustre extension that had been added to the building in the 1960s. Some of them travelled a long way to spend their weekends working here. Jim Wreland had come all the way from Gloucester. A former oil fields engineer who spent 25 years in Libya, he recently married someone from that cathedral city some distance up the M5. 'My uncle was the longest-serving signaller at Exeter West,' he told me proudly as the sun gleamed on the earring piercing one of his lobes. 'And my grandfather was a driver on the Great Western.'

'So three generations of our family have loved trains,' put in his son Alan. 'Make that four, because my son will too when he's old enough.' Alan still lived in Exeter, which sounds a hop, step and a jump compared to Gloucester but was still some 45 miles away. Most weekends David and Linda Swallow made that journey too. 'Sometimes I don't want to get out of bed on a Sunday morning,' admitted Linda, 'but once I'm here I forget about any problems at home. It takes me away from the real world.'

Away from the real world and into the rail world, you could say. Not a bad place to be on a Sunday morning, with a magnificent viaduct at hand and the prospect that one day it might – just might – be part of a line that would once again connect two towns separated by nigh-on 20 miles of the most glorious countryside in all England. 'I like to think that we're contributing, in a small way,' said David, 'to something that's going to be big.'

16

THE NARROW-GAUGE RAILWAY

REFLECTIONS FROM THE WAITING-ROOM

What I'd heard during my weekend in Devon had been inspirational. Not just from those Trust members who had a dream, but also from the volunteers who gave up so much of their spare time to try to help make that dream a reality. Think again if you thought the spirit of Tom Rolt and Alan Pegler was dead. Rolt led the resurrection of the Talyllyn line – what you might call the first great 'Railway Adventure', to quote the title of his book – and Pegler the Ffestiniog, in those grim post-war days when Britain had lost its place as a premier world power and a post-Imperial world beckoned. We now live in a post-industrial world. The mines and mills, factories and furnaces that Rolt and Pegler took for granted have long gone. So have the steaming railways that connected them.

For the most part, that is. The narrow-gauge lines that had been resurrected, largely but not entirely in remote parts of the UK, had been built initially on the whims of wealthy men and the backbreaking efforts of those they'd paid to get the job done. What you might call the resurrect-ors had usually not been paid. They'd done it for a variety of reasons, sometimes intertwined – the need to get out and do something, a feeling of being part of a major project, wanting to help revive part of our collective past, to learn more about engineering, or simply to get into the cabs of venerable steam trains with fascinating working histories.

Certainly I'd seen a desire to get close to those engines among many who'd visited these railways, and not just among those old enough to remember when steam trains ran on the main line. During my narrow-gauge travels I'd met people of all ages and both sexes who'd become fascinated by a precious part of our history. And while I may have sometimes cursed the lengthy journeys to visit those lines, I'd revelled in meeting most of their passengers as well as the volunteers and indeed the paid staff who kept them running.

Just as enjoyable had been sitting back to savour the scenery beyond the windows – confirmation that, when viewed from a little train, this small island still has breathtaking variations in landscape, a marked contrast to the corporate and municipal uniformity that has taken hold of large parts of our towns and cities. But then, unlike so many of our towns and cities, rural landscapes have remained largely unscathed by the turbulence of our industrial and war-faring history (not to mention the soullessness that settled on so many post-war council planning departments). And those parts of the landscape that were 'scathed', particularly by mining, have largely been blended back into their natural surroundings, adding layers of fascinating industrial history in the process.

Those contrasts in landscape had struck me forcibly when I found myself travelling through the gently undulating countryside of East Anglia on the Bure Valley Railway two or three days after being transported through the soaring hills around the South Tynedale. One minute the highest market town in England, the next, the gateway to the Norfolk Broads.

That sense of stepping into a different world had been even more pronounced when, shortly after being in the far southeast of Kent, I finished up in North Wales. More specifically, it was the experience of setting foot on the shingle of Dungeness, Britain's only official desert, watching flocks of strange birds seemingly explode across a vast skyscape – and then, the following weekend, being conveyed 3,560ft up Snowdon by a rack-and-pinion railway modelled on the Swiss cog system used to get passengers to the summit of the Alps.

Were we still on the same small island?

Yes, we were, although it seemed about as unlikely as the history of the Romney, Hythe and Dymchurch railway that had conveyed me to Dungeness: a line founded by a racing driver with an extraordinarily long name, made even longer by the fact that he had been a captain in World War I. But it had been in the 1939–45 conflict that, to quote from a sign in the railway's museum, 'the world's smallest railway became part of the nation's war machine', conveying men, machinery, piping and parts for defence mechanisms to the edge of England. It was, after all, a vital link with the battlefields of Normandy.

Plus ça change, as they say across the Channel. Not much more than two decades earlier narrow-gauge railways had played a vital part in moving men to the trenches on the Western Front. Or so I'd discovered at Leighton Buzzard, where much of the track had been acquired from the bloodiest battlefields in human history. Armour-plated engines that had survived World War I finished up transporting sand from the quarries to the brickworks.

Remnants of our Imperial past were to be found on any number of the lines that I'd visited. Particularly Statfold Barn in Staffordshire, where the open days attracted not only enthusiasts from all over the UK but train drivers, too. One of them, I recall, was excited by the prospect of getting behind the controls of engines that had worked in South Africa and Fiji, Indonesia and India. In South Africa they had usually been used on sugar plantations; in India it could have been anything, anywhere. After all, some of those plucky little workhorses had made it to the summit of British hill stations.

That was part of their appeal to entrepreneurs who set up these oddball lines in unlikely parts of the UK. Narrow-gauge railways could get to the parts that others couldn't. Seemingly impossible gradients could be surmounted. Mountains could be wound around and passes passed between. Towns could be by-passed around the edges.

Standard gauge, on the other hand, was so much less flexible, more direct. Always has been. George Eliot's greatest novel, *Middlemarch*, is set against the background of the laying-down of those pioneering railways in the 19th century. Some panjandrum would plan one venture or another by drawing a line across a map, and anything in the way would have to be flattened. Part of the novel focuses on the apprehension this transport revolution was arousing in villages and small towns that happened to be in the way.

For Middlemarch then read Middle England now, as villagers from the Chilterns to rural Warwickshire look at the plans for HS2 with a mixture of nervousness and indignation. The former Chancellor George Osborne was fond of portraying his pet project as an example of the 21st century connecting with the 19th – showing the world that we could still get things done, like our Victorian and Edwardian forebears. Money and muscle got things done.

That was the case on narrow-gauge lines as well, albeit on a much smaller, more local scale. They were set up to get things done in out-of-the-way places. For the most part, that is. In some cases it was difficult to discern any economic logic behind their existence. The Leek and Manifold line, with its grandiose engine and rolling stock, closed in 1934, having lasted just 30 years. As one of the navvies who had worked on it apparently observed, 'It started in nowhere and finished in nowhere'. Very attractive nowhere, mind you, in the wilds of north Staffordshire. In fact, it transported milk some 8 miles or so before around three hundred churns were sent on the main line all the way to London. It couldn't last, and it didn't. The end of the dairy was very soon followed by the end of the line.

And no, it hadn't reopened as a leisure line, despite the stunning surroundings. As we know, many others have – in some cases against almost insurmountable odds. Back in the summer I'd found myself in Kent, on the line that ran between Sittingbourne Viaduct and Kemsley Down. There used to be another station in between, at Milton Regis. Until, that is, vandals had not only burnt down the buildings but also painstakingly smashed up the platform with a crowbar. What a contrast between the dedication to destruction displayed by the moronic thugs who had plagued that line and the selflessness of the many active volunteers who gave up so much of their time to keep it going.

In Britain we've always had a soft spot for the underdog, the hitherto unheralded battler against the odds. And that, I suppose, goes right to the heart of the appeal of narrow-gauge railways. They were underdogs as well as oddballs, but they could reach places that their big brothers on the main line couldn't. One end of the Sittingbourne and Kemsley Light Railway was surrounded by a retail park that could have been anywhere in the UK – or, indeed, anywhere in the US. But the railway itself, in the face of such adversity, preserved a little passageway into a past that was unique to this small corner of England.

Perhaps the most ambitious resurrection of a railway long ago written off as a white elephant had been the Welsh Highland. The slate industry was past its peak and the line had lasted just 13 years. Admittedly, the Ffestiniog had kept it going, still losing money, until the start of World War II. Then, 50 years after the end of the war, the Ffestiniog had started the lengthy process of bringing it back again. Granted, there was a lottery grant of £4.3 million, but still all sorts of bureaucratic obstacles had to be overcome. Over 20 years further on and the Welsh Highland can now promote itself as 'the longest heritage railway in the UK'. What's more, it was making even more money than the Ffestiniog, connecting as it does Porthmadog with the magisterial walled port of Caernarfon, after a journey of two hours and 25 minutes on which you could even enjoy a hot meal while also feasting your eyes on breathtaking scenery.

In other words, it now goes where visitors want to go and provides them with the sort of service they've come to expect. For all our ongoing economic woes, far more of the public has time and money on its hands than in the days when a vast empire was under British rule. And, yes, from the hills and valleys of North Wales to the much lower Bure Valley in Norfolk, there are narrow-gauge railways professionally run and making profits from what is now oxymoronically known as the leisure 'industry'.

But there were many more lovers of these lines who helped to keep them going for no financial recompense whatsoever. They gave up their spare time, sometimes travelling considerable distances to work as drivers, guards, firemen or just to help out with the maintenance of engines and rolling stock. Most, but not all, were men. Men who still liked being in sheds and getting their hands dirty. Men who not only loved trains but also discovered a particular affinity with the maverick, quaint and eccentric nature of narrow-gauge railways in particular. In some ways, it seems, we have more in common with our Victorian and Edwardian forebears than we imagine.

Or so I mused on the last of my lengthy journeys, to a place even more remote than most. North of the border this time, with another distinctive landscape, and a somewhat undignified if exhilarating adventure at the end of the line.

17

THE TWO SANTAS

THE LEADHILLS AND WANLOCKHEAD RAILWAY

It was an eventful Saturday morning, to put it mildly. Bizarre might be a better description. At one point I had found myself scaling an extremely steep railway embankment, clinging on for grim death to a piece of jutting rock, losing my footing and questioning my sanity. Later I had been almost bent double as I shuffled tentatively down a tunnel into a lead mine that closed in 1830. At the far end, enthroned in a fairy-lit grotto, was Father Christmas.

Perhaps I should begin at the beginning...

I was in Leadhills, to be precise, high up in Lanarkshire, west of the highest point on the West Coast Main Line at Beattock Summit as it hurtles through Scotland towards Glasgow. It was the last month of the year and I was here to visit my last narrow-gauge railway, and certainly one of the most out-of-the-way.

Even before I'd reached the railway my trip had taken on a surreal air. Having got out at Sanquhar Station on the Carlisle-to-Glasgow line I'd checked in at the Hopetoun Arms in Leadhills, named after the laird here on the Lanarkshire side of the county border and been shown to a spacious room with a particularly opulent bathroom: Prince Charles had apparently stayed there once as a guest of the laird. Very reasonable, too, as it turned out. So why, when I came to settle up, did I greet the figure at the bottom of the bill with such a sharp intake of breath? *Where had those brandies come from?*

Then it started to come back to me… I'd finished that Friday evening in the bar talking about Scottish football, as you do, with a former semi-pro who, like Marlon Brando in *On the Waterfront*, 'coulda been a contender' – if it hadn't been for the cruciate ligament damage, that is. The wee drams were mine; those brandies had been his!

Leadhills: the clue's in the name. The hills around the village are still embedded with veins of lead. Zinc, too. There was some gold in 'them thar hills' as well, and the Museum of Lead Mining at nearby Wanlockhead still offered a five-hour course in gold-panning – as well as an annual opportunity to meet Santa after a short journey on a narrow-gauge railway.

Lead mining in these parts went on for many centuries. Until the 1930s, that is, when the bottom fell out of the industry with a dull thud. It wasn't just the

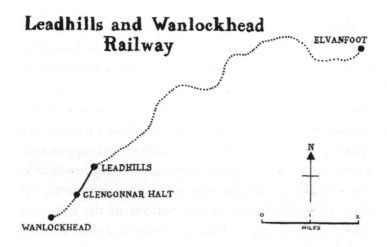

Leadhills and Wanlockhead Railway

mines that closed. The train that ran on the Caledonian Railway's main line from Leadhills to Wanlockhead, and on to Elvanfoot, ground to a halt. There was no longer any lead to be transferred to another train and sent on to the port on the east coast at Leith to be shipped to Holland. As for the track, that was ripped up in 1945 – the end of World War II, of course. Was it also the end of the line?

Not quite. Just over 40 years later, a stretch of track was re-laid. Only three-quarters of a mile, mind you. And this time the gauge was 2ft, as opposed to 4ft 8½in. The man who inspired those volunteers back in the mid-1980s was one Alastair Ireland, a local bank manager and railway enthusiast who has since died. 'He was the engine that drove the revival of the line,' I'd been told over a pint and a wee dram or two in the Hopetoun bar earlier on that Friday evening by Martin

Hollingworth, one of the few volunteers on the Leadhills to Wanlockhead Railway who lived locally. Except it didn't run all the way to Wanlockhead. Not yet, anyway. There were plans to extend the line by another half a mile. That would take it as far as Radar Road, so named because it provided access to what looked like a giant golf ball but turned out to be a vital part of the radar system for Glasgow Airport. Also, some of the residents currently had a right of way to the trackbed for access to their properties.

Saturday morning dawned chilly but bright. I walked off some of a substantial full Scottish breakfast en route to Leadhills Station, and the first volunteer that I got talking to there turned out to be a former solicitor who was now the secretary of the railway society and a man with good news to impart. 'At midnight,' Harvie Paterson proclaimed, 'we were granted a lease of £1 a year for 25 years by the Duke of Buccleuch.'

It was all lairds and lead round here. The Buccleuchs had long held sway on the Dumfries and Galloway side of the county border that divided the two villages once united by a railway. And, for some time, plans to extend the line back to Wanlockhead had been held up by one of the Duke's tenant farmers. 'He retired in June,' Harvie went on, 'and nobody in his family wants to take on the farm. So we can now get on with something that we've wanted to do for 18 years. At some point in the future, we hope to extend it further.'

Ticket issued on last day of the Caledonian Railway, 1939

Wanlock, *1931*

All the way back to Elvanfoot?

'Well, that's some 6 miles from here. So perhaps not in my lifetime, nor the lifetime of anyone here. It might have been easier if British Rail hadn't blown up a viaduct in 1991 – an act of vandalism in my humble opinion.'

So why did they do it?

'An early onset of health and safety. Still, we recovered some of the bricks for the construction of our signal box.'

Just beyond the box were two houses, one built for the former stationmaster and the other for a train driver.

'They were the highest houses in Scotland,' I was told by Paul Chennock, who was going to be driving a succession of trains at regular intervals throughout the weekend. Two even higher houses had since been built in Wanlockhead, some 1,500ft above sea level.

It was all very confusing for an Englishman who had been told that he was in the so-called Lowlands. Wasn't Ben Nevis, in the Highlands, the highest mountain in the British Isles?

'There are no houses at the top of Ben Nevis,' said Paul. His Dublin accent was unsullied by years of living in Cumbria. Like many a volunteer here, he thought nothing of driving considerable distances when required. Very few of them lived locally. All the more remarkable then that, in the summer of 2016, a railway that mostly ran at weekends only put on a regular daily service when the B797 between Leadhills and Wanlockhead was closed for resurfacing.

Yes, this was a rare case of a train replacing the bus. Apart from the Hopetoun Arms and a historic Miners' Library, there was not a lot in Leadhills – apart, that is, from a shop and a doctor's surgery. So here was a case of a narrow-gauge railway adapting itself from a visitor attraction to become a vital community service. For a short period, at least.

Some five months on, and it was time for something that is part of the narrow-gauge calendar all over this small island: the Santa Special. I was booked on the 10 o'clock but, since I'd arrived an hour earlier, Paul offered me the chance to travel on a trial run. This was to be the train's first outing since the Halloween Special and, as he put it, 'We need to check that everything's OK.'

At least there was no snow blocking the line today. 'We had 2ft of it up here one Easter,' Paul confided. Well, as many a sign informed us, we were at an altitude of 1,498ft, making this the highest narrow-gauge 'adhesion' railway in the UK.

As on Snowdon, the engine was at the back on the way up, and at the front on the way back. But the gradient was nowhere near as steep as that tackled by Snowdon's rack-and-pinion system, so no jagged cog-wheels were required to get a grip on the track. 'All adhesion means is that the friction between the wheel and the rails is what keeps the train going,' Paul explained.

But didn't the engine keep it going?

'Yes, but when the line gets steeper, the wheels can start to slip.'

Particularly when there were leaves or ice on the line, presumably. Certainly there was ice on the rudimentary wooden platform at Glengonnar Halt at the end of our journey. Paul and his colleague Darren Welsh lugged out heavy bags of grit to spread around. No-one wanted one of the kiddies to slip over while posting a letter to Santa near a sign warning that 'Passengers leaving this platform area do so at their own risk'. Too right, as I would discover later in the morning.

The 1.5-mile ride from Leadhills to Glengonnar and back took 45 minutes, most of it at a stately 4 to 5 miles an hour. Plenty of time, then, to take in the surroundings. The landscape had a certain other-worldly quality. It was more like a moonscape than a landscape. There was plenty of grass – but it was flat, windswept grass with patches of so far un-melted snow nestling in crevices here and there. Swathes of brownish heather bordered the line and the grouse moors. I travelled at the front in both directions – in the brake van with Darren on the way out, and in the considerably warmer engine with Paul on the way back.

When he was not working on the railway, Darren ran a bookshop in Moffat. 'It's 20 minutes away down the next valley,' he told me in an accent that owed more to northern England than the Lowlands of Scotland, before leaping off to open a gate barring our way across a track covered with a greyish stone. There was a lot of it about. Greyish stone, I mean. 'It's spoil from the mines,' Darren confirmed, pointing to the left where the natural hills were complemented by partially grassed-over spoil, and to the right where the remains of the old mine washeries were built from the same stone that had been hacked away to get at the lead. Lairds and lead again: those grouse moors were still visible behind us.

Back at Leadhills Station, excitement was mounting. Families were arriving in the car park. Some children were already running up and down the platform, waiting to board one of the two carriages between the brake van and what looked a bit like Thomas the Tank Engine. It turned out to be a diesel built in 1975 for the National Coal Board. 'We have two steam engines,' Martin Hollingworth had told me: 'one built by Orenstein and Kopel and the other by Decauville.' I'd tried to look suitably impressed. 'They're over 100 years old, both privately owned, and both in bits.'

The chances of them being reassembled at Leadhills Station seemed fairly remote, judging by the engine shed. Compared to other sheds I'd been shown it was a little on the small side. There was a chance, Harvie Paterson told me, of building a new one soon. Money would be forthcoming from one of the wind farm companies that evidently needed to spread some goodwill in the light of the hostility to its presence from many of the locals. As they say in many another part of the UK, it's an ill wind farm that blows nobody any good...

Both the carriages on the Santa Special were decorated with baubles and tinsel. One had windows; the other was more exposed to the elements. I found myself in the latter, sitting opposite the Bridgwood family, sensibly clad in woollen hats. Well, not *too* sensibly in the case of nine-year-old James, who was sporting a hat designed to look rather like a penguin's head. 'We live about 15 miles away and come on this line regularly because we love the scenery,' said his mother, Sarah.

'And the trains,' put in his father Derek. Or it might have been Eric. I didn't like to keep asking as he had a quiet voice, and the noise from the diesel engine was surprisingly loud as it throbbed through the wide-open window frame through which Harvie was thrusting sheets of paper and envelopes. 'I don't have a pen, I'm afraid,' he added.

'Use mine,' I said, handing it over to James's sister Isobel. She twizzled it around somewhat tentatively. 'Not sure what I want for Christmas,' she murmured shyly. No such hesitancy with James. He planned to ask Santa for a fire extinguisher. 'He wants to be a fireman when he grows up,' whispered his father.

Harvie and other volunteers were waving us off. One was sporting a splendid pair of antlers atop his woolly hat, and there were model reindeer, penguins and polar bears attached to odd pieces of fencing along the track, much to the delight of Isobel. 'She's finally decided to ask Santa for a Lego board,' Sarah explained, handing back my much-twizzled pen.

At Glengonnar the Bridgwood kids joined the queue to post their letters in a temporary post box that had been set up at the far end of the now ice-less platform. First in line was a little girl who told me she wanted a pair of *Thomas the Tank Engine* pyjamas. 'She loves engines,' said her proud father. 'Takes after her dad.'

Strange to think that somewhere around here were the remains of the Glengonnar mine, where minerals were first extracted in the 1450s. There would no doubt be plenty of information about all the mines at the museum at Wanlockhead. That's where Father Christmas would be waiting for the families who were soon re-boarding the train back to Leadhills. There they would pick up their cars and drive to the grotto.

I didn't join them because I didn't have a car. Instead, I'd decided to walk to Wanlockhead. It wasn't *too* far, I'd been told: all I had to do was stroll down the road above us. Quite a way above us, by the look of it.

There were two choices. I could clamber up a somewhat steep railway embankment and risk falling flat on my face in front of a train-load of adults and children. 'Or you could walk on down the cutting,' Darren had told me. 'Eventually it winds round and

An old shot of Leadhills station with advertisement posters

Caledonia Railway goods ticket, 1892

connects with the road. The trackbed might be a bit boggy, though.'

So I walked on, walked on with hope in my heart and mud on my shoes. Not too much mud: it was a bit soft underfoot, but not boggy enough to stop your intrepid correspondent. There was plenty of that grey stone about. Quite a few rocks as well, embedded in the embankment that seemed to become steeper with every step. Eventually I approached the bend, expecting to see the road ahead. Instead I saw bogs. Big bogs. Well, sizeable puddles anyway, topped by a thin film of ice. How deep were those puddles?

I had no intention of finding out. The alternative seemed preferable, even if it meant scaling the embankment. A particularly hefty piece of rock was jutting out halfway up. If I could cling on to that and haul myself up, surely I wouldn't be too far from the summit?

Slowly but surely I clambered onward and upward. Muddy ledges in the grass provided the footholds. Until, finally, I touched the rock – only to lose my faltering grip when one of the ledges gave way.

The bad news was that I slipped down the embankment to the detriment of my stylish if somewhat ancient overcoat. (Austin Reed, if you please, and so old that it was made in England.) The good news was that I didn't slide all the way to the bottom, and I narrowly missed a substantial pile of sheep dung.

An old song by Jerome Kern that my parents used to sing came to mind, about picking yourself up, dusting yourself off and starting all over again. It wasn't just bloody-mindedness that kicked in. There was no alternative, apart from icy puddles of dubious depth.

This time I got a proper grip on the rock, first with my fingers and then with my feet. What's more, the grassy ledges towards the summit were not so muddy, and hence not so slippery. When I finally ducked under the fence at the top and trod on reassuring tarmac, I felt as though I'd just scaled Ben Nevis. Muddied but unbowed, I walked on to Wanlockhead. The sun had made an appearance over one of the many hills hereabouts and the worst was behind me.

Ahead was the long and winding road to the Museum of Lead Mining, which I found eventually at the far, or rather the bottom, end of a steep village full of smoking chimneys and barking dogs. The only human beings I caught sight of on the way were a white van man and a couple unloading their car near a sign in capital letters reading NO MORE WIND FARMS.

Inside the museum shop was a somewhat demented Santa, waving his arms about. On closer inspection he turned out to be a life-sized model, electronically powered. The real thing was easier to discern once I'd stepped outside again and been pointed in the right direction. A hundred yards or so down a babbling brook and across a wooden bridge was a small group of museum staff, and a figure whose red garb seemed all

Rispin Cleugh viaduct, built in 1891 by Sir Robert McAlpine & Co

Demolition of Rispin Cleugh viaduct with explosives, 1991

305

the brighter by contrast with the grey stone surroundings of the disused mine.

His real name turned out to be Alec Brown, but don't tell the kids that. 'I'm double-booked today,' he told me in the broadest Scottish accent I'd heard all day. 'Have to be in another grotto in Penpont this afternoon.'

Tom Gardiner, who did maintenance at the museum, was ready to step into the breeches of Santa this afternoon. Not to mention the boots, beard, jacket and hat, under which he would presumably tuck the greying pony tail that was currently dangling down from under his yellow hard hat.

'I've also done a stint as Father Christmas before now,' confided John Evans, chairman of the museum's trust. 'A frightfully posh boy from Castle Douglas came up to me and said, "We've come on the train, you know." So I responded: "Would that have been first class, young man?" He looked a bit puzzled, but his dad started to smirk. When I asked the boy what he wanted for Christmas, he casually asked for a Land Rover.'

'A Dinky-type Land Rover, presumably?'

'No, no. "I'd like a real one," he said. So I told him: "Do you know a little boy came in earlier asking for a quad bike?"

'"Oh, really?"'

'"Yes," I said. "And he's not getting that, either."'

The families from the 10 o'clock train were coming bounding over the bridge, headed by a little girl with very few teeth but 'a whole list of things' to ask Santa for.

Donning the regulatory helmet, I followed the Bridgwood family into the mine, and we adults ducked our way in to that magical grotto. As I'd discovered in many a mine hitherto, even a man of just under 6ft had to keep his head down, his back bent and his knees braced. The height can vary within a few feet, and this tunnel was no exception. Despite my crouched posture, I still managed to bring about that resounding crack to the cranium on one occasion. Had it not been for that helmet, my head would have had a gash like the slit on the top of a piggy-bank.

The kids had to wear helmets as well, despite there being little chance of them banging their heads. Isobel's was perched somewhat precariously atop her woolly hat. As for James, he had removed his penguin hat to leave surprisingly long locks dangling from the rim of yellow plastic.

'What did you get from Father Christmas?' I asked when we were out in the open air again.

'A mermaid colouring book,' replied James, a little disgruntled. 'He thinks I'm a girl.'

'You need to get that hair cut,' grinned his dad. He kindly offered me a lift back to Leadhills Station, and I jumped at the chance of a short cut to what turned out to be a mince pie and a restorative glass of mulled wine in the Leadhills engine shed.

Later – much later – I was on a Virgin Pendolino heading south, and beginning to feel a little peckish. Breakfast and that mince pie now seemed a long time ago. The public address system was *bing-bong*-ing even more than usual. There were lengthy delays south of Preston (overhead lines), and south of Wigan (signalling problems). The joys of mainline travel. Had it only been that morning that I'd been clambering up an embankment and edging down a lead mine? It seemed like another time in another country.

ACKNOWLEDGEMENTS

When my former publisher Graham Coster suggested a book on the UK's narrow-gauge railways, I was a bit sceptical at first. 'Isn't that a bit "anorak-ish"?' I suggested. Quite wrongly, as it turned out. So thanks to Helen Brocklehurst, Rebecca Needes and their team at the AA for commissioning the book, as well as to Graham for pushing it my way, and for his advice and knowledge as well as his skills as an editor.

Little did I know when I embarked on my travels around this small island how much fun the research would turn out to be. From the south of England to the Lowlands of Scotland, from North Wales to East Anglia, I've enjoyed not only the widely varied views from the windows but also chatting to fellow passengers on trains, on platforms, in cafes, ticket offices and station shops. Almost all have been open, friendly, good-humoured and more than happy to talk. There were far too many of them to mention here.

I would, though, like to list some of the names of those who keep these lines going, those who have resurrected them against the odds and those who are still struggling to do so in the face of bureaucratic planning laws and opposition from a few residents. Some of those mentioned below are professionals who manage or promote the railways, drive or fire the trains.

Then there are the volunteers who give up much of their spare time to keep these lines running, as drivers, firemen, guards, ticket office clerks or someone who cleans out the toilets. There are some who have done all those jobs. Others still do. Thank you too to all those who helped in supplying pictures and memorabilia with which to illustrate the book.

So here we go, in no particular order of priority...

Leighton Buzzard Railway: Terry Bendall, Mervyn Leah, John Hopper, William Shelford, Jamie Randall.

Sittingbourne and Kemsley Light Railway: Paul Best, Jacqueline Shanks, Martin Staniforth.

Romney, Hythe and Dymchurch Light Railway: Danny Martin, Zac Clark, Rob Fagg, Alex Ross.

Ffestiniog Railway: Andrew Thomas, Alan Heywood, Mike Todd.

Snowdon Mountain Railway: Alan Kendall, Paul Baker, Amanda Ward, Robert Jones.

Talyllyn Railway: Ian Drummond, John Scott.

Vale of Rheidol: Will Smith, Sophia de Rochefort, Chris Harris, Jack Smith.

Welsh Highland Railway: Andrew Thomas (again), Keith Frazer.

Statfold Barn: Graham Lee, Carol Lee, Paul Ingham, Nick Noon, Leanne Noon.

Leek and Manifold Valley Light Railway: Rebecca Simcock, Jeannette Mellor.

Ravenglass and Eskdale Light Railway: Peter van Zeller, Jackie Pharaoh, Simon Garrod, Lisa Braithwaite.

South Tynedale Railway: Stuart Hines, Steve Hopper, Martin Ashley.

Bure Valley Railway: Andrew Barnes, Susan Munday, David Lowe, Roger Danes, Matt Howard.

Southwold Railway: John Bennett, John Ridgway, David Lee.

Lynton and Barnstaple Railway: Dave Tooke, Tony Nicholson, Nigel Thompson, Jim and Alan Wreland, David and Linda Swallow.

Leadhills and Wanlockhead Railway: David Wimpenny, Harvie Paterson, Martin Hollingworth, Paul Chennock, Darren Welsh, John Evans and Alec Brown, otherwise known as Santa Claus.

I found the following books of particular use in writing mine:

L T C Rolt, *Railway Adventure* (Newton Abbot, David & Charles 1977; first published 1953) – about the revival of the Talyllyn

J B Snell, *One Man's Railway: J E P Howey and the Romney, Hythe and Dymchurch Railway* (Newton Abbot, David & Charles 1986)

John Winton, *The Little Wonder: 150 Years of the Festiniog Railway* (London, Michael Joseph, revised edition 1986)

The History Press now publish *Railway Adventure*, and have kindly given permission to reproduce the extracts in Chapter 6.

DIRECTORY OF RAILWAYS

Leighton Buzzard Railway
Page's Park Station
Billington Road
Leighton Buzzard
Bedfordshire, LU7 4TN

www.buzzrail.co.uk
Telephone: 01525 373888
International: +44 1525 373888
Email: station@lbngrs.org.uk

Sittingbourne and Kemsley Light Railway
Sittingbourne Viaduct Station
PO Box 300
Sittingbourne
Kent, ME10 2DZ

www.sklr.net
Information line: 01795 424899
International: 44+ 1795 424899

Romney, Hythe and Dymchurch Railway
New Romney Station
2 Littlestone Road
Littlestone
New Romney
Kent, TN28 8PL

www.rhdr.org.uk
Telephone: 01797 362353
International: +44 1797 362353
Email: info@rhdr.org.uk

Ffestiniog and Welsh Highland Railways
Harbour Station
Porthmadog
Gwynedd, LL49 9NF

www.festrail.co.uk
Telephone: 01766 516000
International: +44 1766 516000
Email: enquiries@ffwhr.com

Snowdon Mountain Railway
Llanberis
Gwynedd, LL55 4TT

www.snowdonmountainrailway.co.uk
Telephone: 01286 870223
International: +44 1286 870223
Email: info@snowdonrailway.co.uk

Talyllyn Railway
Wharf Station Tywyn
Gwynedd, LL36 9EY

www.talyllyn.co.uk
Telephone: 01654 710472
International: +44 1654 710472
Email: Enquiries@talyllyn.co.uk

Vale of Rheidol Railway
Park Avenue
Aberystwyth
Ceredigion, SY23 1PG

www.rheidolrailway.co.uk
Telephone: 01970 625819
International: +44 1970 625819
Email: info@rheidolrailway.co.uk

Statfold Barn Railway
Open on three Enthusiasts' Days a year; attendance by pre-requested invitation only via website.

Statfold Barn Farm
Ashby Road
Tamworth
Staffordshire, B79 0BU

www.statfoldbarnrailway.co.uk
Telephone: 01827 830871
International: +44 1827 830871

Leek and Manifold Valley Light Railway
Walking and cycling route of the Manifold Way, which includes much of the trackbed of the old railway:
www.thepeakdistrict.info/derbyshire-cycling/manifold-way
www.theaa.com/walks/the-manifold-way-420974

Ravenglass and Eskdale Railway
Ravenglass
Cumbria, CA18 1SW

www.ravenglass-railway.co.uk
Telephone: 01229 717171
International: +44 1229 717171
Email: steam@ravenglass-railway.co.uk

South Tynedale Railway
The Railway Station
Station Road
Alston
Cumbria, CA9 3JB

www.south-tynedale-railway.org.uk
Talking timetable: 01434 382828
Telephone inquiries: 01434 338214
International: +44 1434 338214
Email: enquiries@south-tynedale-railway.org.uk

Bure Valley Railway
Aylsham Station
Norwich Road
Aylsham
Norfolk, NR11 6BW

www.bvrw.co.uk
Telephone: 01263 733858
International: +44 1263 733858

Southwold Railway
27 High Street
Southwold
Suffolk, IP18 6AD

www.southwoldrailway.co.uk
Telephone: 01502 725422
International: +44 1502 725422
Email: mail@southwoldrailway.co.uk

Lynton and Barnstaple Railway
Woody Bay Station
Martinhoe Cross
Parracombe
Devon, EX31 4RA

www.lynton-rail.co.uk
Telephone: 01598 763487
International: +44 1598 763487

Leadhills and Wanlockhead Railway
The Station
Leadhills
Lanarkshire, ML12 6XS

www.leadhillsrailway.co.uk
Email: secretary@leadhillsrailway.co.uk

INDEX

IMAGE CREDITS

The Automobile Association would like to thank the following photographers, companies and picture libraries for their assistance in the preparation of this book.

Abbreviations for the picture credits are as follows – (t) top; (tl) top left; (tr) top right; (b) bottom; (bl) bottom left; (c) centre; (cr) centre right; (AA) AA World Travel Library.

Book Block
Endpapers Courtesy of F&WHR; 20(t) Heritage Image Partnership Ltd / Alamy Stock Photo; 20(b), 38(b), 202(t), 257(t), 275(b) Chronicle / Alamy Stock Photo; 23(t), 23(b), 84(t), 84(b), 94(t), 94(b), 140(t), 140(b), 147(t), 147(b), 154, 157(t), 157(b), 160(t), 160(b) Courtesy of F&WHR; 38(t), 43 ©Kevin Lane; 51(t), 51(b), 181, 193(t), 193(b), 202(b), 227(t), 227(b) Reproduced by kind permission of the RCTS photographic archive; 61, 64(t), 64(b), 71(t), 71(b), 72(b) Courtesy of RH&DRA Heritage Group Collection; 72(t) Trinity Mirror / Mirrorpix / Alamy Stock Photo; 107(t), 107(b), 112, 118 Courtesy of Snowdon Mountain Railway; 124, 131(t), 131(b), 134(t) Courtesy of TR Collection; 134(b) Courtesy of W.A. Camwell; 196 Courtesy of Graham Coster; 209 Clarence O. Becker Archive / Alamy Stock Photo; 230 Milepost 92 1/2 ; 239(t), 239(b), 246 Courtesy of Bure Valley Railway Archive collection; 257(b) The Keasbury-Gordon Photograph Archive / Alamy Stock Photo; 275(t) Courtesy of Lynton and Barnstaple Railway; 295(t), 295(b), 302(t), 302(b), 305(t), 305(b) Courtesy of Leadhills and Wanlockhead Railway Archive

Plate Section
1(t) Worldwide Picture Library / Alamy Stock Photo; 1(b) ©Gordon Edgar; 2(t) Roger Bamber / Alamy Stock Photo; 2(b), 3(t), 3(cr), 3(br), 8(b), 9 Courtesy of F&WHR; 3(bl), 16(t) Courtesy of Chris Arnot; 4 AA/Steve Lewis; 5(tl), 5(tr) Courtesy of Snowdon Mountain Railway; 5(b), 6(b) Courtesy of D. Turner; 6(t) Courtesy of TR Collection; 7(t), 7(b), 8(t) Courtesy of John R. Jones; 10(t), 11(t), 16(b) ©Gordon Edgar; 10(b) Milepost 92 1/2; 11(b) AA/Neil Coates; 12(t) AA/ Peter Sharpe; 12(b), 13(t) Courtesy of Ravenglass and Eskdale Railway; 13(b) Cumbriastockphoto / Alamy Stock Photo; 14(tl) AA/M Birkitt; 14(tr), 14(c) Courtesy of Malcolm Pettitt/BVR Collection; 14(b) Julia Gavin UK / Alamy Stock Photo; 15(t) Courtesy of Tony Nicholson; 15(b) Courtesy of F&WHR/Steve Broomfield

Every effort has been made to trace the copyright holders, and we apologise in advance for any unintentional omissions or errors. We would be pleased to apply any corrections in a following edition of this publication.